PURE LAINE

THREADS
OF
SEGUIN FAMILY HISTORY

MARC PHILIP SEGUIN

ONTARIO HISTORY
PRESS
2025

© Copyright 2025 Marc Seguin

All rights reserved.
No part of this publication may be reproduced, stored in a retrieval system or transmitted in any form by any means, electronic, mechanical, photocopying, recording or otherwise without the prior written permission of the author.

The dynamic nature of the Internet may result in web addresses or links contained in this book to change and they may no longer be valid after publication.

ISBN: 978-1-7387801-4-3

Ontario History Press
Prince Edward County, Ontario, Canada
2025

Comments and inquiries can be sent to the author: press@ontariohistory.ca
This book is available through local bookstores and online retailers or by contacting the author.

Other books by Marc Seguin:

Pure Laine: The Lineage of Two Seguin Families, Theodore Seguin and Alphonsine Seguin (2024)

The Last Nine Standing: A Landlubber's Guide to the Last Remaining Lighthouses on the Canadian Shores of Eastern Lake Ontario (2022)

Farewell to Canada: The Last Imperial Garrison and Canada's First Permanent Force 1867-1871 (2021)

For Want of a Lighthouse: Guiding Ships Through the Graveyard of Lake Ontario 1827-1914 (2nd ed., 2019)

The Cruise of the Breeze: The Journal, Art and Life of a Victorian Soldier in Canada (2018)

Cover design by Marc Seguin

The cover depicts a portion the traditional *ceinture fléchée* worn by *Canadiens* since the 17th Century and often patterned after the original sash from the region of Assomption, Quebec.
This symbol of French Canada was later co-opted by the Métis Nation.

• Table of Contents •

Preface	1
A Note on Sources	4
Dit Names, Spelling Variations and Place Names	6
The Lineage Charts	9
Lineage Chart Symbols and Abbreviations	10
Introduction	13
Indigenous North American Ancestors	15
Emigrants From Europe	20
The Founding of Montreal	23
The *Filles à Marier* and *Filles du Roi*	26
Soldiers 1665-1783	28
Colonists vs. Natives	41
Villains and Victims in New France	47
Dispelling the Catholic Myth	50
Le Pays d'en Haut and *Le Détroit*	53
Into the 20th Century and Beyond	65
Appendices	
Appendix A - Summary Lineages	77
Appendix B - Francois Seguin's Arrival in Canada	98
Appendix C - A War of 1812 Research Project	100
Appendix D - List of dit names	102
Bibliography	109
Index of Family Names	111
General Index	119

• List of Tables •

Table 1 Ancestors of *La Grande Recrue*, 1653   25

Table 2 Arrivals at Montreal, 1659   26

Table 3 Ancestors who were *Filles du Roi*, 1663-1673   27-28

Table 4 Ancestors in the Carignan-Salières Regiment
        and Attached Companies   34

Table 5 Ancestors in th *Troupes de la Marine*, 1683-1759   37

Table 6 Ancestors Killed or Captured by Iroquois, 1648-1709   43

Table 7 French Calvinist Ancestors in New France, 1649-1667   52

Table 8 Migrants to the Detroit River Region and
        the Upper Country   58-59

Preface (2025)

In February, 2023, I started this family history as a very small research project; trying to uncover any documentary evidence of my Indigenous ancestry. However, the project quickly ballooned into what became a massive, 660 page volume which was published in 2024 under the title *Pure Laine: The Lineage of Two Seguin Families*.

Going back as far as the late 16th Century, that volume included details of more than 3,500 individuals with some 800 different surnames listed on more than 500 pages of Lineage Charts and notes summarizing the family tree of my paternal grandparents, Theodore Seguin and Alphonsine Seguin. It also included ninety pages of introductory remarks, appendices and narrative essays illustrating some of the "threads" of my Seguin ancestors' past that I uncovered over the course of many months of research.

In an attempt to make this history of two of the many Seguin families in North America more accessible to the general reading public, I have excerpted the narrative essays (with some revisions) from the original volume to create this book. I have left out most of the Lineage Charts and present only the threads of Seguin family history that make up the myth of "*pure laine*".

Marc Philip Seguin
August, 2025

Although the original Lineage Charts are not included in this book, they are marked throughout as (Ch. *n*) where *n* is the chart number. For reference purposes, a searchable version of the lineage charts can be viewed and downloaded at www.ontariohistory.ca/seguin.pdf .

See page 9 for details about searching the Lineage Charts.

The original volume, *Pure Laine: The Lineage of Two Seguin Families*, containing the narrative and all of the charts, can also be ordered from your local bookstore or purchased online at Chapters/Indigo (www.indigo.ca).

Preface to *Pure Laine: The Lineage of Two Seguin Families* (2024)

Initially, I had no intention of compiling a comprehensive family tree of my paternal grandparents, Theodore Seguin and Alphonsine Seguin, extending back to the 17th Century. Rather, this started in February, 2023, as very small research project into the aboriginal ancestry of my predecessors. That was a few years after I had my DNA analysed by two different companies: 23andMe and Ancestry. Results from both of these companies showed that about 1% of my ancestry composition was Indigenous North American. This could mean that, as few as seven generations ago, I had an ancestor who was a native person. This was not a complete surprise to me since my mother, Loretta E. Ouellette (1929-), had always told me and my siblings that one of her ancestors — probably one of her great-grandmothers — was "a full-blooded Indian". My mother also had her DNA tested and it showed that she too had about 1% Indigenous North American ancestry.

The biggest surprise came with the DNA results from my father, Philip E. Seguin (1929-2015). He also had 1% Indigenous North American ancestry. This was completely unexpected and it was the first hint that our "pure" French ancestry, the "*pure laine*" of Seguin family lore, was, perhaps, more myth than reality!

I then started a search for documentary evidence of this native ancestry along both my maternal and paternal lines. In the process of tracing my complete ancestry, I had the idea that my children, Philip R. Seguin (b.1997) and Daniel C. Seguin (b.1999), might, some day, be interested in some of the family history that I was uncovering. However, I realized that to give my sons a complete picture of their ancestry, I would also have to include the family lineages of my mother (the Ouellettes, Blays, Groulxs, Lauzons, etc.) as well as those of my wife, Marjorie Cluett (the Cluetts, Bodmans, Moreheads, McMillans, etc.). I thought I could, without too much difficulty, trace most branches of all of these families back to the first immigrants to North America and produce a genealogy reference book for my sons. That started me on a project that quickly took on overwhelming proportions.

By the time my research had taken me back ten generations, I had compiled basic birth, marriage and death details for almost 2,000 individuals who were direct blood ancestors of my sons. It was only then that I realized that, for some branches of these family trees, there would still be another four generations to add before arriving at the first European immigrant ancestors. Since each past generation contains twice as many ancestors as the previous one, this would mean that I had to gather information on at least another 20,000 individuals! Not only was this a formidable research task but, given the page layout to which I was limited (which could show no more than fifteen individuals on each page, plus notes), the size of the resulting book would be in excess of 3,000 pages!

It also occurred to me that, perhaps, some of my siblings and some of my 1st-cousins on my father's side might be interested in the Seguin portion of my research. My father,

Philip, and his older brother, Leonard, used to joke, with some air of pride, that they were "*pure laine*" — that they had pure French ancestry. This idea was in no small part due to the fact that both of their parents were from Seguin families separated by six generations. Their father, Theodore, was the son of Napoleon Seguin. Their mother, Alphonsine, was the daughter of Philippe Seguin *dit* Laderoute. Unknown to them at the time of their wedding, Theodore and Alphonsine were 5th-cousins.

In compiling this genealogy, my hope is that it will be of some interest to those who have chosen to open its pages, and that it might inspire readers to look deeper into their own families' histories.

Marc Philip Seguin
February, 2024

Acknowledgements

I would like to thank my aunt, Aline Wanne (*née* Seguin), for donating her collection of genealogy books to me. Father Denissen's two-volume set has been especially useful in compiling the Lineage Charts. I would also like to thank my late cousin, Michelle Mailloux, the daughter of Antoinette Mailloux (née Seguin) and Patrick Mailloux, whose collection of Seguin family material was passed along to me.

For her patience and diligence editing and proofreading multiple drafts of the manuscript for this book, I would like to thank my wife and partner of 30 years, Marjorie Cluett Seguin.

> A work of this kind can never truly be complete.
> Names and places and dates will always be missing.
> Any comments, corrections, additions or other suggestions
> will be gratefully received: press @ontariohistory.ca

A Note on Sources

The majority of the research material used to compile this book consists of reliable secondary sources; that is, work by other historians and genealogists. The use of primary source material — original church records, census data, cemetery records, etc. — has been limited largely to that which was available online via the internet. The most useful published sources and online databases are mentioned here. A complete bibliography can be found on page 109. Source references that appear in the text are enclosed by square brackets [...].

Online Sources

• Programme de Recherche en Demogaphie Historique (PRDH) (www.prdh-igd.com)
This has been used as the primary source for genealogical information for Quebec families. This is a computerized database developed by the University of Montreal which is available by subscription. It includes all available birth, death and marriage records relating to every person who lived within the present boundaries of the Province of Quebec between 1620 and 1850. This is an invaluable resource for anyone researching French-Canadian genealogy and it contains links to digitized source documents at Généalogie Quebec (www.genealogiequebec.com). For a complete list of sources used to compile this database, refer to the PRDH bibliography page (www.prdh-igd.com/en/bibliographie).

Unfortunately, the geographical and temporal limits of this database make it difficult to research French-Canadians who were born or died outside of Quebec or who were born or died outside of the system's date limits. Also, researchers must be aware that the PRDH computer program has taken the numerous spelling variations of family names and normalized them. This has sometimes resulted in names that do not match the names shown in many of the original documents.

• WikiTree (www.wikitree.com)
This is a great site for French-Canadian genealogy. Too often, publicly available and editable genealogy websites (like the family trees on ancestry.ca) contain a great deal of conflicting and completely undocumented information which makes them quite unreliable as sources of family history. However, most of the French-Canadian family names found on WikiTree are extremely well documented; many listing sources that can be viewed online.

• Archiv-Histo (archiv-histo.com/pionniers.php)
• Fichier-Origine (www.fichierorigine.com/recherche?)
Both of these databases provide reliable but limited information on the early French immigrants to Canada.

A Note on Sources

Published Sources

• Denissen, Christian. *Genealogy of the French Families of the Detroit River Region, 1701-1936,* rev. ed. Detroit, 1987.

This has been used as the primary source for genealogical information for French families in the Detroit/Windsor region. This is a 2-volume set, which picks up geographically where PRDH leaves off, providing a fairly thorough listing of French-Canadian families that lived in the Detroit River region between about 1704 and 1900. It also traces many family lineages back to France. It is available online:

    Vol.1, https://archive.org/details/genealogyoffrenc01deni
    Vol.2, https://archive.org/details/genealogyoffrenc02deni

• Fournier, Marcel & Langlois, Michel. *Le Régiment de Carignan-Salières: Les Premières Troupes Françaises de la Nouvelle-France, 1665-1668.* Montreal, 2014.

Many books have been written on this subject, and this one gives a very good summary of the soldiers of the French Army who arrived in Canada in 1665.

• Gagné, Peter J. *Before the King's Daughters: The Filles à Marier, 1634-1662.* Florida, 2002.

This is the most comprehensive study of the *filles à marier*. This book is limited in its availability, but it can be found at some academic libraries or purchased online at a number of sites including https://globalgenealogy.com/countries/canada/quebec/resources/602501.htm. An online list summarizing the *filles à marier* in Gagné's book can be found at https://www.tfcg.ca/filles-a-marier-en.

• Landry, Yves. *Orphelines en France, Pionnières au Canada: Les Filles du Roi au XVII Siècle,* 2nd ed. Quebec, 2013.

Several books have been written on the subject of the *filles du Roi*, but authors do not agree on a definitive list of names. However, this is one of the most scholarly works on the subject and it contains an extensive list of names along with biographical information. One online list of names of many of the *filles du Roi* can be found on WikiTree. [www.wikitree.com/wiki/Project:Filles_du_Roi#Our_Lists_of_Filles_du_Roi_.2F_Nos_listes_de_Filles_du_roi]

• Seguin, André. *Seguin Dictionnaire Généalogique, 1672-2005,* 2nd ed. Boucherville, Que., 2005

This is the standard reference of almost every Seguin descended from Francois Seguin and Jeanne Petit between 1671 and 1999. It provides only limited information on female ancestors.

• Tanguay, Cyprien. *Dictionnaire Généalogique des Familles Canadiennes.* Montreal, 1886.

This important multi-volume work has been used by French-Canadian genealogists for more than a century. It is available online: https://archive.org/details/dictionnaireg01tang.

Dit Names, Spelling Variations and Place Names

The first ancestor to arrive in North America bearing the Seguin name was Francois SEGUIN "*dit* Laderoute". *Dit* means "called" or "known as". The *dit* name is a nickname. So, Francois SEGUIN was also called "Laderoute" (*la deroute*, translated as "the rout", a decisive defeat in battle). Some French immigrants arrived in North America with nicknames that had long been associated with their families in France. Others obtained their nickname only when they were in the French Army or only when they arrived in North America. Some *dit* names were passed from a father to his children for many generations. Others were passed from a mother to her children.

The nicknames could be related to a person's place of origin like Pierre GARMAN *dit* Picard who was from the Picardie region of France, or Pierre MIVILLE *dit* Le Suisse who was from Switzerland. They might describe a man's trade like Claude DESJARDINS *dit* Lecharbonnier (the charcoal maker) or Louis GUERTIN *dit* Lesabotier (the clog maker). They are sometimes associated with a physical characteristic like Jean MIGNERON *dit* Petit Jean who could have been a very small man or, perhaps as a twist on his physical stature, he might have been very large. Sometimes the nickname was just a play on the person's surname like Jean-Baptiste LEFORT *dit* Laforest (the forest) or Pierre MARSAN *dit* Lapierre (the stone). The significance of many *dit* names has been lost.

In many cases, the *dit* name was dropped altogether or went out of usage in some branches of the family, but not in others. Some *dit* names eventually supplanted the surname altogether. In the case of Jean-Baptiste MALBOEUF *dit* Beausoleil who arrived in New France C.1690, his *dit* name was passed down several generations to his great-grandson, Augustin. However, there is no record of Augustin's daughter, Julie BEAUSOLEIL, ever using the name Malboeuf. Now, in some parts of Canada, the name Beausoleil is very common but the name Malboeuf is almost non-existant. This also happened with some branches of the Seguin family where LADEROUTE became the legal surname.

In other cases, different *dit* names were attached to different generations of the same family. This happened with Pierre GUILLET *dit* Lajeunesse who arrived in New France, C.1642. His son, Louis, was known as GUILLET *dit* Cinqmars. Complicating things further, some *dit* names were associated with several different surnames. Examples of these include BOYER *dit* Lafontaine, ROBERT *dit* Lafontaine, MENARD *dit* Lafontaine and PERRAS *dit* Lafontaine. The *dit* name Lafleur is associated with no fewer than nine surnames of the direct ancestors of Theodore and Alphonsine.

There were more than 200 different *dit* names used by the ancestors of Theodore Seguin and Alphonsine Seguin. Many of those names along with their associated surnames are listed in *Appendix D*.

While the use of surnames plus *dit* names certainly complicates matters when researching French Canadian genealogy, a greater challenge comes from the lack of standardized spelling of names. Most Seguins have encountered variations on the spelling of our name — "S E Q U I N" being the most common mis-spelling. The database of the Program de Recherche en Démographie Historique (PRDH) developed at the University of Montreal has identified more than thirty variations of the Seguin name used in documents from the 17th, 18th and 19th centuries. Part of the reason for this is the difficulty sometimes encountered when trying to decipher the handwriting that appears in official documents. Most priests and court clerks had terrible handwriting. Another reason is that names were often spelled phonetically — the way they sounded, with no regard to standardization. This has given us spellings like "Saiguin" and "Sayen" among many others. In some cases, early official documents consistently show one spelling of a family name, but later documents consistently show another similar but different spelling.

Also, the PRDH database has further complicated the spelling issue by using a computer algorithm to normalize the variations of a surname found in the original source material. This has sometimes resulted in a computer-generated "standardized" name which may not be found anywhere in the original church records, census forms or legal documents.

Alternate spellings for some family names have been included in the notes accompanying many of the Lineage Charts.

Another challenge for genealogists dealing with French ancestors is the sometimes confusing array of place names. A birthplace or place of marriage or burial location in France often includes the name of the town (*village*), parish (*paroisse*) and province. However, another record for the same person or an entry created by another genealogist might include the name of the town, diocese (*évêché*) and/or arch-diocese (*archévêché*), the sub-province (*pays*), district (*arrondisement*) and/or province, and even the name of the region or the more modern geographical division that replaced the province after the French Revolution, *le département*.

For example, an individual born in the city of La Rochelle, France, might appear in one record as being from Ste. Marguerite, Aunis — St. Marguerite being the name of one of the many parishes in La Rochelle, and Aunis the name of the province. Another record might show the same individual born in La Rochelle, Charente-Maritime.

7

Charente-Maritime is the modern *département* in France. The birthplace of Francois SEGUIN *dit* Laderoute appears in the PRDH database as the town of St. Aubin en Bray, diocese of Beauvais in the province of Picardie. Other birth records for Francois show he was born in the district of Beauvais in the *département* of Oise, which is the modern designation of the region where he was born. Both of these are correct as both are the same place with different names given to them at different periods in history.

These variations in the use of place names can make it difficult to confirm the accuracy of the lineage of individuals. Whenever possible, multiple sources have been used to confirm that the lineages in this book are as accurate as possible. Comments, suggestions or documented corrections to the lineages that are presented here can be sent to the author.   marc@ontariohistory.ca

THE LINEAGE CHARTS

The Lineage Charts contained in the original volume, *Pure Laine: The Lineage of Two Seguin Families*, are referenced in this book as (Ch.*n*), where *n* is the chart number. Those charts can be viewed and downloaded at www.ontariohistory.ca/seguin.pdf .

SEARCHING THE LINEAGE CHARTS — For example, to search the charts for a Lineage Chart such as **(Ch.187-4)**, enter the search term "Chart 187" (including quotation marks), then find the page shown as **CHART 187** and look for person number **4)** on that chart.

BLANK PAGES — These pages relate to the lineages of families that are part of a larger genealogy and not directly related to Theodore Seguin or Alphonsine Seguin. Therefore, they have been left out.

MISSING NAMES, DATES, PLACES — At the time the lineage charts were compiled, some information for certain individuals could not be found. It is hoped that future genealogists will be able to provide this missing data.

NOTES — Brief notes concerning many individuals are included with most charts. References in square brackets [...] are given as an aid to more in-depth research. *Dit* names and some alternate spellings are also included with the notes.

Key to Reading the Lineage Charts

	CHART 23		
	Cusson Fevrier *dit* Lacroix Fissiau *dit* Laramée Froment Hamel Lacroix *dit* Roberge Morisseau Vegiard *dit* Labonté		Current chart number with list of family names found on that chart.
	FROM CHART 3		The previous chart in the lineage for the families shown on the current chart.
VI	VII	VIII	Generation numbers in Roman numerals. Generation I includes the children of Theodore and Alphonsine Seguin
	4) Father (of 2)		Person number (eg. 4) and relationship to the previous person (eg. Father of person 2)
	ent SEGUIN[3]		Superscripted numbers (eg. 3) refer to notes on the opposite page.
	cont. on CHART 166		Next chart in the lineage for this family

LINEAGE CHART SYMBOLS AND ABBREVIATIONS
(see Lineage Charts at www.ontariohistory.ca/seguin.pdf)

*	*dit* name ("called", or a nickname)
≈	Emigrated from Europe to North America
f^m	*Fille à marier*
f	*Fille du Roi*
‡	Indigenous North American
Δ	Migrated to the Detroit River region or the Upper Country (*le Pays d'en Haut*)
↑	See above
↓	See below
†	Soldier
[...]	Source reference
b.	born or baptized
cont.	continued
C.	circa
Ch.	Chart (eg, Ch.2-8 = Chart #2, person #8)
Cty	County
d.	died or buried
Eng.	England
J.B.	Jean-Baptiste
M.	Marie
m.	married
N/A	A series of charts which are Not Applicable to this genealogy
Ont.	1867 to present – Province of Ontario in the Dominion of Canada
	1841 to 1867 – Canada West (part of the British colony of the United Province of Canada)
	1791 to 1841 – British colony of Upper Canada
	1774 to 1791 – part of the British colony of Quebec
	1763 to 1774 – part of the British colony of Canada
	1605 to 1763 – part of the French colony of Canada (New France).
Que.	1867 to present – Province of Quebec in the Dominion of Canada
	1841 to 1867 – Canada East (part of the British colony of the United Province of Canada)
	1791 to 1841 – British colony of Lower Canada
	1774 to 1791 – part of the British colony of Quebec
	1763 to 1774 – part of the British colony of Canada
	1605 to 1763 – part of the French colony of New France (Canada).
Twp	Township

Pure Laine

Threads
of
Seguin Family History

Introduction

In our Western, Euro-centric culture, our family name is usually passed down to us from our father. As a result, most family genealogies trace only the paternal branches of a family tree — our fathers, grandfathers and great-grandfathers — while making only peripheral mention of the maternal line — our mothers, grandmothers and great-grandmothers — the women without whom none of us would be here. This Seguin genealogy is not just limited to those bearing the "Seguin" name. Instead, ALL paternal and maternal ancestors of Theodore Seguin and Alphonsine Seguin have been considered (their direct ancestors only; no siblings, aunts, uncles or cousins of their direct ancestors). The original volume, *Pure Laine: The Lineage of Two Seguin Families,* contains much of the narrative that appears in this book, but it also contains Lineage Charts listing more than 800 different family names, every one of which has contributed directly to the DNA — the bloodline — of Theodore Seguin or Alphonsine Seguin (or both of them)*.

Alphonsine Seguin, grew up in the early 20th Century on a farm near the largely French-speaking community of Tecumseh in Essex County, Ont., Canada, not far from Windsor, Ont. and Detroit, Michigan. Her ancestors had lived in the Detroit/Windsor region since her 3rd-great-grandfather, Joseph SEGUIN, had arrived at the wilderness settlement of Detroit from the Montreal area around 1750.

Theodore Seguin, grew up in the town of Thurso, Que., in the Ottawa River valley. His 3rd-great-grandfather was Joseph's brother, Pierre SEGUIN; making Theodore and Alphonsine 5th-cousins (see *Appendix A-1*).** It was Joseph's and Pierre's grandfather, Francois SEGUIN *dit* Laderoute, who, in 1665, was the first ancestor bearing the Seguin name to arrive in North America from Europe.

Alphonsine was sometimes known to declare that she was "...not just a Seguin..." but "... a Seguin *dit* Laderoute!", adding the ancient nickname by which the family had been known since at least the time Francois SEGUIN left France for the New World. This fierce pride in her family and its French roots was coupled with her deep religious faith and belief in the teachings and rites of the Roman Catholic Church. Most, if not all of her six children, having grown up in this environment of unapologetic, French-Canadian family pride, would often half-jokingly say that they were "*pure laine*" — they were from pure Roman Catholic, French stock; genetically as pure as the finest wool.

---

* The Lineage Charts can be viewed and downloaded at *www.ontariohistory.ca/seguin.pdf*.
References to specific Lineage Charts appear in parentheses (Ch.*n*).
Source references appear in square brackets [...].

** Theodore and Alphonsine were also 6th-cousins-once-removed through their common ancestors, Pierre Mallet (b.1629) (Ch.74-2) and Marie Anne Hardy (Ch.74-3). See *Appendix A-2*.

With so many previous generations of French-Canadians behind them and, indeed, with both of their parents descended from distantly-related Seguin families, the myth of "*pure laine*" held by many Seguins is understandable. However, the historical and genealogical research presented here shows that while the fabric of the lineage of Theodore Seguin and Alphonsine Seguin is <u>mostly</u> wool, it is <u>not</u> 100% pure wool. Strands of English, Swiss, German, Belgian and Indigenous North American ancestry, together with pagan and Protestant Puritan and Calvinist threads had been woven into their genetic background, the result of which is a rich and diverse fabric that all Seguins can be proud to wear.

Indigenous North American Ancestors

While the myth of "*pure laine*" would have it that all of Theodore Seguin's and Alphonsine Seguin's ancestors originated in France or, at least, that they were all European, this is not the case. The DNA test done by the author's father, Philip E. Seguin (son of Theodore and Alphonsine), shows that he has approximately 1% Indigenous North American ancestry. This would be true for his five siblings as well. Documentary evidence shows that, in this Seguin line, there are no fewer than five Indigenous North American ancestors from several different Indigenous groups who married European spouses and whose children have passed their DNA on to all of their descendants. The predecessors of these Indigenous North Americans are also Seguin ancestors and, all told, make up a portion, however tiny, of the bloodline of Theodore and Alphonsine.

‡ Gisis BAHMAHMAADJIMIWIN, called Jeanne (Ch.444-7). (see *Appendix A-3*)

This Anishinaabe Nipissing (*Nepisnguée*) woman was Theodore Seguin's 8th great-grandmother (on his mother's side). Gisis was born around 1602 in the Lake Nipissing area of what is now Ontario, Canada. Sometime before 1628, she was "married" to one of Samuel de Champlain's interpreters, Jean NICOLET, who lived among the Nipissings for several years. She died around 1628, shortly after giving birth to her daughter Marie Madeleine Euphrosine NICOLET (Ch.123-13).

Nipissing Warrior, 1717.
[Bibliotheque Nationale de France, IFN-7804362]

Her father then took Marie Madeleine to Quebec City to be educated at the Roman Catholic convent school run by the Ursuline nuns. In 1663, Marie Madeleine married Elie DUSSAULT (Ch.123-12), a sailor, newly-arrived from France. Elie had been baptized into the Calvinist Church at La Rochelle, France, but he must have converted to Roman Catholicism before the marriage as the wedding took place in Quebec City's Notre Dame Catholic church, and their four children were all baptized into the Catholic faith.

‡ Ouchistaouichkoue, called Marie OLIVIER or Marie SYLVESTRE. (see *Appendix A-4*)
This woman was Alphonsine Seguin's 7th-great-grandmother (on her mother's side). Marie was probably born around 1625, at the St. Joseph mission at Sillery, Que., just outside of Quebec City. Her father, Roch MANITOUABEOUICH, was Wendat (Huron), and her mother, Outchibahanoukoueou, was Wabanaki or Algonquin. On the wishes of her father, Marie was adopted by one of Champlain's interpreters, Olivier Tardif, so that she could be educated at Quebec City and Christianized. Marie married the Parisien, Martin PRÉVOST at Quebec City in 1644. This was the first officially recorded marriage in New France of a European man and an Indigenous North American woman. Marie died in 1665, three months after giving birth to her 8th child, Marie Therese PRÉVOST (Ch.176-5).

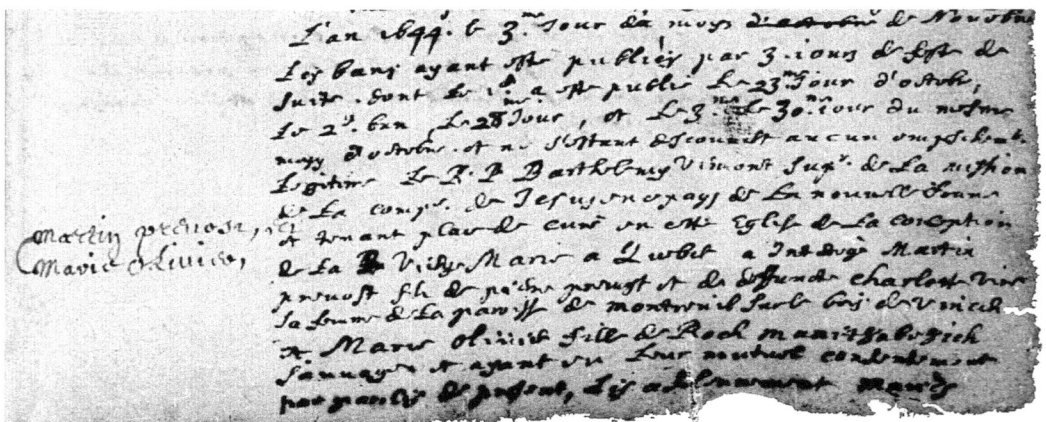

Marriage register, Martin Prévost and Marie Olivier, "*fille de Roch Manitouabeouich.*"
November 3, 1644. [Paroisse Notre-Dame-de Quebec. Drouin Collection.]

‡ Marie Madeleine ST. JEAN *dit* Lavallée (Ch.149-7). (see *Appendix A-5*)
This Haudenausonee Onondaga (*Onontague*) woman was Alphonsine Seguin's 6th-great-grandmother (on her father's side). Marie Madeleine was born around 1672 in Onondaga (Iroquois) territory south of Lake Ontario. She may have been captured as a child by a Wendat or Anishinaabe raiding party and then traded to the French at Montreal where she was brought up by European parents, Jean Sabourin and Marie

Gaillard. She was given the Christian surname St. Jean. [www.wikitree.com/wiki/Onontagué-1] In 1689, at Montreal, Marie Madeleine married Francois FRANCOEUR *dit* Lavallée (Ch.149-7). She died at Quebec City in 1700.

Marriage register, Francois Francoeur and Madeleine St. Jean (*Magdeleine St. Jean d'onontague*). November 25, 1689. [Notre-Dame-de Montreal. Drouin Collection.]

‡ Jean-Baptiste PRÉVERT (or PRÉVOST) (Ch.95-2). (see *Appendix A-6*)

This Pawnee (*Panis*) man, was Theodore Seguin's 5th-great-grandfather (on his father's side). Born around 1680, in the Platte River region of present-day Nebraska, Jean-Baptiste was likely captured as a child by the Santee Dakota Sioux (Isanyathi) or by the Anishinaabe Potawatomi and sold to French fur-traders as a slave.

Over the course of many centuries, the Pawnee had been forced north from the Gulf of Mexico by the Apache, to eventually occupy territory in the central plains of North America where they became the enemies of the tribes already established there. The Caddoan-speaking Pawnee were largely a sedentary people who built permanent villages of sod-covered earth lodges, and they spoke a language separate from the Siouan- and Anishinaabe-speaking tribes that had long been established in the region. [see George Hyde, *The Pawnee Indians*] Pawnee captives were often taken by enemy tribes and sold as slaves to the French. This occurred so often that, in the 18th Century, *Panis*, the French name for the Pawnee, became synonymous with the word slave, even if the enslaved person was not from the Pawnee nation.

A Pawnee Family
[Detail of an engraving after Seth Eastman, "Pawnees at the Morning Star Sacrifice Ceremony". From Henry R. Schoolcraft, *The Indian Tribes of the United States*. Philadelphia, 1884. plate 62.]

Almost 3,000 enslaved Indigenous North Americans appear in the historical record of New France and the subsequent British colony of Quebec between 1689 and 1796. [see Marcel Trudel, *Canada's Forgotten Slaves.*] However, in the late 17th Century, when Jean-Baptiste PRÉVERT was likely enslaved, there were fewer than forty *Panis* recorded in Canada (the actual number was likely much higher). The owning of slaves in New France was an accepted practice throughout the 17th Century, but it was not until 1709 that slavery was codified into law.

It was when he was still quite young that Jean-Baptiste PRÉVERT was likely brought to Montreal where he was Christianized and probably given his freedom. In 1710, he married Marie Genevieve DESFORGES and together they had 5 children. [PRDH]

Jean-Baptiste likely spent most of his adult life working in the fur-trade and, by 1725, he had moved his family to Detroit. He died two years later, somewhere in the "Illinois Country" or elsewhere in area known as *le Pays d'en Haut,* the Upper Country — the vast region west of Montreal where beaver and other fur-bearing animals still flourished in large numbers.

Marriage register, Jean-Baptiste Prévert (*Sauvage de la nation des panis*) and Marie Genevieve Desforges. November 16, 1710.
[Notre-Dame-de Montreal. Drouin Collection.]

‡ Nicolas DOYON *dit* Laframboise (Ch.157-6) (see *Appendix A-7*), another Pawnee (*Panis*) man was Alphonsine Seguin's 6th-great-grandfather (on her father's side). Nicolas was born in the Platte River region of Nebraska, probably around 1684. Like Jean-Baptiste PRÉVERT, he also may have been captured as a child by an enemy of the Pawnee and sold to French fur-traders as a slave. At age 14, records show that Nicolas was in Quebec City, the slave of a man named Doyon whose name he took when he married Marie Louise GAREAU (Ch.157-5) at Boucherville, Que., in 1710. They had 8 children together, including Marie Josephte DOYON (Ch.157-3). Nicolas worked as a blacksmith at Boucherville until his death in 1727.

Marriage register, Nicolas Doyon and Marie Gareau. July 28, 1710.
[Ste. Famille parish, Boucherville, Que. Drouin Collection.]

In addition to these five direct ancestors with whom Theodore or Alphonsine share DNA, there are five other European male ancestors whose first or second marriage was to an Indigenous North American woman. While Theodore and Alphonsine have no DNA connection with these women, they share a cultural connection with them, and any of their children would be distant Seguin half-cousins:

‡ Dorothée Sauvagesse (Wendat or Montagnais), 1st wife of Francois PELLETIER *dit* Antaya (Ch.174-6), *m.* 1660, at Tadoussac, Que. No issue.

‡ Marie Gonnentenre (Oneida), wife of Charles Garman "Gannonchiase" (son of Pierre GARMAN, Ch.174-10), *m.* C.1665, in Oneida territory. Issue, 1 daughter. At age 10, Charles had been captured by the Iroquois, along with his father, during a raid on Trois-Rivières, Que., in 1653. His father was killed, but Charles was adopted into an Oneida clan.

‡ Marie Francoise Picarouiche (Anishinaabe), 1st wife of Pierre LAMOUREUX *dit* St. Germain (Ch.101-6), *m.* 1664. Issue, 3 children.

‡ Anastasie Illinoise (Illinois nation), 2nd wife of René DAIGNEAU (Ch.88-2), *m.* 1705, at Detroit. Issue, 1 daughter.

‡ Francoise Cunegondé Cardinal (unknown Indigenous tribe or nation), 2nd wife of Pierre TABEAU (Ch.113-6), *m.* 1714, at Montreal. Issue, 7 children.

Emigrants from Europe

The first European ancestor of Theodore and Alphonsine to arrive in North America bearing the Seguin name was Francois SEGUIN *dit* Laderoute (Ch.72-6), from the French province of Picardie. Francois was born July 4, 1644, at Saint-Aubin-en-Bray, a small rural village eighty kilometers north of Paris in the Beauvais region of the province of Picardie. He was the first child of Laurent SEGUIN and Marie MASSIEU. It is generally accepted that Francois arrived in Canada in 1665 (see also *Appendix B*). He likely sailed from France aboard the ship *La Justice*, as a soldier in the Carignan-Salières Regiment which had been dispatched to New France to fight the Iroquois and force them to make peace with the French colonists, the *Canadiens*. After being discharged from military service, he settled in Canada, and in 1672, he married Jeanne PETIT (Ch.72-7), a 16-year-old *fille du Roi* from La Rochelle, France, who had just arrived in the colony. This was the beginning of the Seguin family name in North America. However, by tracing the complete family lineage of Theodore Seguin and Alphonsine Seguin through all of their paternal and maternal branches, we find that more than 300 of their direct European ancestors had already established themselves in New France over the course of the previous sixty years.

La Nouvelle France (New France), the general term applied to the collection of North American colonies established by the French over the course of the 17th Century, included *la Terre Neuve* (Newfoundland), *l'Acadie* (Nova Scotia and New Brunswick), *le Canada* (Quebec and Ontario) and *la Louisiane* (the region centred around the Mississippi River valley down to the Gulf of Mexico). From 1604 to 1663, various private companies were chartered by the kings of France to administer these colonies, giving them exclusive trading rights and authority over all commercial and settlement activities. The most well known of these companies was *la Compagnie de la Nouvelle France*, also called *la Compagnie des Cents-Associés* (the Company of One Hundred Associates), chartered in 1627. While the primary objective of these companies was always to make money for their investors — most commonly by participating in the lucrative fur-trade with the Indigenous populations — they also had an obligation to establish permanent settlements and recruit tradesmen and families to colonize the French possessions in North America.

Louis HÉBERT (Ch.463-4 & Ch.485-14), as an employee of one of the early trading companies, was the first European in the Seguin family tree to set foot in North America. He was one of Alphonsine Seguin's 8th-great-grandfathers (on her father's side) (see *Appendix A-8*) and one of her 9th-great-grandfathers (on her mother's side). Louis HÉBERT came to North America on three separate occasions. He arrived first in 1606, at Port Royal in Acadia (near present-day Annapolis Royal, Nova Scotia) but went back to France the following year. He would then return to Port Royal for two years starting in 1611. Six years later, he arrived at the site of present-day Quebec City where Samuel de Champlain, had established a small settlement with its *"Habitation"*, a wooden, castle-like fortified structure of four buildings built on the banks of the St. Lawrence River in 1608. Champlain had been employed by several of the early trading companies to explore parts of North America in order to find suitable locations for the establishment of commercial bases of operations. He had sailed along the Atlantic seaboard of North America as far south as Cape Cod and had been involved, in 1604, in the short-lived settlement on St. Croix Island, on the Maine/New Brunswick border near the Bay of Fundy. The following year, he also helped to establish the settlement at Port Royal on the other side of the Bay of Fundy, in Acadia (Nova Scotia). In 1627, Champlain was one of the first investors in *la Compagnie des Cents-Associés*.

Louis HÉBERT settled permanently at Quebec City in 1617, with his wife Marie ROLET and their three children. Louis had been trained in France as an apothecary and at Quebec City he cultivated many of the medicinal plants that he used in an attempt to ease the suffering of his fellow colonists. He is considered to be Canada's first successful European farmer. Sadly, a fall on the ice in 1627, ended his life. [http://www.biographi.ca/en/bio/hebert_louis_1E.html]

Meanwhile, in 1613, Nicolas MARSOLET *dit* St. Agnan (Ch.484-6) had arrived in North America. He was one of Alphonsine Seguin's 8th-great-grandfathers (on her mother's side). He had been recruited in France by Champlain to work as an interpreter and intermediary among the Montagnais peoples of the Saguenay River region in New France. It is quite probable that Marsolet had a Montagnais wife and he may have fathered children before going back to France in 1637 to marry Marie BARBIER (Ch.484-5). After Quebec City was captured by the Kirke brothers in 1629 at the end of the Anglo-French War (1627-1629), most of the French inhabitants were transported back to France. However, Marsolet and as many as twenty other French colonists, including Marie ROLET (Louis HÉBERT's widow) and her children, remained in New France. Nicolas MARSOLET continued working in the fur-trade, now in the hands of

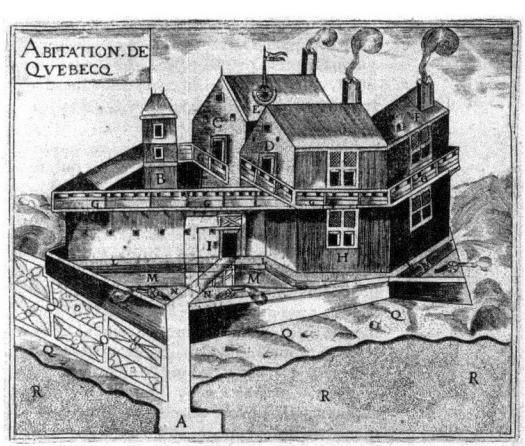

Champlain's *Habitation*, 1613.
[From Samuel de Champlain, *Les Voyages du Sieur de Champlain*. Paris, 1613, p.187. Library & Archives Canada, 3919911]

the English who occupied Quebec City until 1632. While he was considered by some to be a traitor because he had worked alongside the English for three years, Marsolet was exonerated and he later settled with Marie BARBIER at Quebec City where they raised their ten children. [http://www.biographi.ca/en/bio/marsolet_de_saint_aignan_nicolas_1E.html]

The first European Seguin ancestor born in North America was also the first European child born in New France. This child was Hélène DESPORTES (Ch.141-15 & Ch.491-7) (see *Appendix A-8 & A-9*). Her parents, Pierre DESPORTES and Francoise LANGLOIS, had arrived at Quebec City in 1620. Hélène was born that year at the "*Habitation*". However, nine years later, Hélène, along with her parents and most of the other colonists in New France, were forced to leave their homes and go to France after the capture of Quebec City by the Kirke brothers. After peace was restored, many of the exiled colonists returned to New France in 1632. Sadly, in the meantime, Hélène's parents had died in France. In spite of the loss of her parents, Hélène decided to return to the land of her birth. She accompanied her aunt and uncle, Marguerite LANGLOIS and Abraham MARTIN *dit* L'Écossais (Ch.456), 8th-great-grandparents of Alphonsine Seguin (on her mother's side) (see *Appendix A-9*), who were also returning to Canada. Two years later, Hélène married Guillaume HÉBERT (Ch.463), son of Louis HÉBERT, when she was 14 years old in 1634. After Guillaume's death in 1639, she married Noel MORIN (Ch.491) in 1640. As a result of these two marriages, Hélène was both Alphonsine Seguin's 7th-great-grandmother (on her father's side) and 8th-great-grandmother (on her mother's side). [https://www. biographi.ca/en/bio/desportes_helene_1E.html]

The settlers returning to New France in 1632 found Champlain's *Habitation* in ruins, so they had to rebuild the settlement, and many years passed before it began to flourish. Eventually, the settlement developed into the important Canadian city that it is today. Those first colonists to settle at Quebec City are memorialized in a plaque displayed on the city's monument to Louis HÉBERT. Among the ninety-four names inscribed on the plaque, thirty-eight of them are direct ancestors of Theodore Seguin or Alphonsine Seguin.

Plaque commemorating the first European settlers at Quebec City. [Montmorency Park, Ville de Quebec]

In total, approximately 600 individuals in the Seguin family tree emigrated from Europe and settled in the French colonies of North America between 1606 and 1777. While a small number of these emigrants came from England, Switzerland, Belgium and Germany, most came from France; many from the regions of Normandy, Brittany, Perche and Saintonge as well as from the cities of La Rochelle and Paris. The greatest proportion of these immigrants, 400 of them, mostly men, but also some women and children, arrived in New France in the forty year period between 1633 and 1673. The men usually came to Canada as indentured labourers, known as *engagés*, who were contracted to work in the colony for a fixed term at a fixed salary with their food, lodging and return transportation paid for by their employer in New France. While the *engagés* were paid workers, they were also considered the property of their masters and, until the term of their contract expired, they had very few rights — they could not work in the fur-trade, could not enter a tavern, and could not get married. Many were skilled tradesmen and they were usually recruited for a 3-year or a 5-year term. Their occupations included such trades as carpenters, masons, pit sawyers, joiners, wheelwrights, millers, shoemakers, weavers, tailors, blacksmiths, toolmakers and armourers. A large number also worked as servants, farm hands and general labourers.

Some of these early immigrants came as family groups with wives and children accompanying the men. A small number had their families join them at the end of their contract; others had families back in France who they would never see again if they chose to remain in Canada. Those *engagés* who stayed in the colony would usually receive a grant of land which they could clear and farm. However, only about half of all *engagés* chose to stay in New France at the end of their contracts. In 1666, one-quarter of the male population over 15 years of age — 350 individuals — were *engagés*. [Dechêne, *Habitants*, pp.31,34] Of those, only about 175 remained in New France when their contract expired. The overall result was a chronic labour shortage which, combined with the very slow increase in the population, greatly impeded the growth of the colony.

THE FOUNDING OF MONTREAL

From the founding of Champlain's "*Habitation*" in 1608, at what would become Quebec City, until 1663, New France was the domain of private commercial trading companies whose primary concern was the exploitation of the colony's resources for monetary gain. These private companies formed alliances with the Anishinaabe (Ojibway and Algonquin), Montagnais, Wabanaki (Abenaki) and Wendat (Huron) peoples to assist the French in the lucrative fur-trade. Even though the charters of the private companies stipulated that they must recruit substantial numbers of colonists for New France, the settlement of labourers and skilled tradesmen along with a small number of priests and nuns from France, was encouraged only to the extent that it would profit the companies' fur-trading operations. An exception to this was *la Société de Notre Dame de Montréal pour la conversion des Sauvages de la Nouvelle France*, a religious organization that was founded in France in 1639 for the explicit purpose of bringing Christianity to the native peoples in the vicinity of the Island of Montreal.

La Compagnie des Cents-Associés, which had exclusive commercial rights across all of New France, granted the Island of Montreal to *la Société de Notre Dame*. The first fifty settlers recruited by *la Société* arrived on the island in 1642. Theodore Seguin's 7th-great-grandfather (on his mother's side), Léonard LUCOS (Ch.109-10), was among these first settlers, and he is considered one of the founders of Montreal (see *Appendix A-11*). When he arrived on the island, Léonard and his fellow recruits had to clear the land and build a church, a hospital and houses, all surrounded by a palisade for protection from marauding Iroquois. They called their settlement Ville Marie.

After seven very difficult years, Ville Marie was on the brink of collapse from a lack of colonists willing to settle with their families and remain in such a remote and dangerous part of New France. At 120 kilometers distant from the nearest European settlement, Trois-Rivières, Ville Marie was separated from the rest of the French colony by an arduous upriver journey by canoe along the St. Lawrence River. The Island of Montreal was also closer to Iroquois territory making it the target of numerous raids by Five Nations' war parties. The Dutch, who had established their own settlements and fur-trading posts along the Hudson River valley from Fort Orange (Albany, NY) in the north, to New Amsterdam (New York City) in the south, had formed fur-trading alliances with the Five Nations of the Haudenosaunee (Iroquois) Confederacy — the Mohawk, Oneida, Onondaga, Cayuga and Seneca nations. The French had allied themselves with the Wendat, Anishinaabe, Montagnais and Wabanaki peoples. Both European powers used their Indigenous North American allies as proxies to fight for control of the North American fur-trade. This bloody commercial and ethnic rivalry continued after the English replaced the Dutch in 1664, and did not end until well after 1760 when New France capitulated to the British Army and much of the French colony was ceded to Britain in 1763, at the end of the Seven Years War.

But in 1649, with the settlement of Ville Marie on Montreal Island about to collapse, the two principal founders of the settlement, Jeanne Mance and Paul Chomedy Sieur de Maisonneuve, returned to France to recruit more skilled tradesmen and their families to populate the settlement. After embarking from the French port of St. Nazaire, the new colonists endured a two-month sea voyage followed by a two-month delay at Quebec City before arriving on Montreal Island in November, 1653, just in time to face their first Canadian winter. This second recruitment effort, known as *La Grande Recrue* essentially saved Ville Marie, and the village slowly grew into the city we know today as Montreal.

Among this new wave of immigrants were at least fourteen Seguin ancestors. These ancestors are among more than 100 individuals who arrived in Ville Marie that year and who are identified on a commemorative plaque erected by the City of Montreal.

Plaque commemorating the 106 European settlers of *la Grande Recrue* [Ville de Montreal, 2008] overlayed with the list of Seguin ancestors who settled at Montreal in 1653.

By 1659, the settlement on the Island of Montreal was still struggling to survive and *la Société de Notre Dame* was bankrupt; it could no longer afford to bring new immigrants from France to help sustain Ville Marie. However, the priests of the newly-formed Sulpician order in Paris had the vision and the means to take over. They formed *la Compagnie de St. Sulpice* and payed to transport and employ another 110 new settlers along with a number of Sulpician priests. Among the passengers were eighteen more ancestors of Theodore and Alphonsine Seguin.

TABLE 2 – ARRIVALS AT MONTREAL IN 1659

Name	Occupation	Chart
Jacques BEAUCHAMP & wife Marie DARDENNE	Carpenter	108 & 424
Marie Elisabeth CAMUS	(*fille à marier*)	170 & 479
Olivier CHARBONNEAU & wife Marie Marguerite GARNIER & child Anne CHARBONNEAU		120 & 125 & 131
Catherine CHARLES	(*fille à marier*)	130 & 455
René CUILLERIER *dit* Léveillé (b.1637)	Labourer	109
Marie Denise LEMAITRE	(*fille à marier*)	92 & 410
Marguerite MACLIN	(*fille à marier*)	136
Pierre MALLET *dit* Malichon (b.1629)		74 & 135
Marie MONIER & child Urbaine HODIAU *dit* Laflêche		134 & 145 & 468
Hugues PICARD *dit* Lafortune *	Carpenter	183 & 510
Marguerite RIBOU	(*fille à marier*)	412
Jean ROY & wife Francoise BOUET		432
Denis VERONNEAU	Labourer	157

* He arrived in 1653 but went back to France. He then returned to Canada in 1659.

The ship, *Le Saint André*, which had been chartered to transport the emigrants, had, for two years, been used as a military hospital ship, but it had never been properly disinfected. This may have been a factor in the illnesses that many passengers contracted during the voyage. Before disembarking at Quebec City en route to Montreal in the summer of 1659, ten of the passengers died, including several children.

THE *FILLES À MARIER* AND THE *FILLES DU ROI*

In addition to labourers, skilled tradesmen and their families, a number of unattached young women were also recruited to help increase the population of Ville Marie and other settlements in New France. These single, unmarried or young widowed women who arrived in the colony between the years 1634 and 1662 are collectively known as the *filles à marier*, the girls to be married. The historian Peter J. Gagné has identified 262 women who came to Canada during this period, sponsored either by a private trading company or one of several religious organizations which paid their passage and offered them the chance of a better life in the colony in exchange for their labour for a fixed number of years. At least fifty of the *filles à marier* are direct ancestors of either Theodore Seguin or Alphonsine Seguin or both.

In 1663, New France came under the direct control of the French government when King Louis XIV revoked the charters of the private trading companies operating in North America. The population of the colony at that time has been estimated at 2,500 people. [Eccles, "Military Establishment", p.2] In order to encourage settlement and to increase its still-sparse population, a new emigration system with royal sponsorship was put in place. Between 1663 and 1673, some 800 unmarried young women, many of them orphans from the streets of Paris, arrived in Canada and married. They were each provided with household goods that would be useful when starting a family in New France, and all of them came with the promise of a dowry from the king of at least 50 *livres* in French silver currency. This group of women has become known as the *filles du Roi*, the daughters of the king. [see Yves Landry, *Orphelines en France*] The household goods along with the dowry would encourage the single men of New France to take one of the *filles du Roi* as a wife. In all, eighty Seguin ancestors were *filles du Roi*, including Francois SEGUIN's wife, Jeanne PETIT (Ch.72-3) who arrived in the colony aboard the ship *La Nativité* in 1672 when she was 16 years old.

TABLE 3 – SEGUIN ANCESTORS WHO WERE *FILLES DU ROI*

Name	Chart	Arrived
Marie Marguerite ARDION	517	1663
Jeanne AUGER	147	1671
Marie BARBANT	106 & 427	1666
Marie Anne BASMONT	170	1673
Marie Etiennette BAUDON	186 & 512	1671
Jeanne BILODEAU	111 & 430	1665
Marie Francoise BIZELAN	78	1668
Marie BLANCHARD	126 & 428 & 448	1667
Jeanne CAILLÉ	83	1670
Marguerite CARDILLON	84 & 128	1665
Marie CHANCY	127	1673
Marie CHARPENTIER	516	1671
Marguerite COLLET	153	1670
Marie Francoise CONFLAND	79.2 & 188	1667
Francoise CURÉ	137 & 460	1669
Marie Claude DAMISÉ	135	1668
Marie DECELLES	156 & 478	1667
Marguerite DELAPLACE	158	1671
Marguerite DESCENE	91	1672
Marie Jeanne DEVEAU	184 & 188	1667
Ambroise DOIGT	119	1669
Catherine DROUET	118	1671
Catherine DUCHARME	93	1671
Barbe DUCHESNE	173 & 495	1671
Catherine FOURIER	165	1670
Marie GAILLARD	126 & 449	1669
Catherine GRANGER	160	1673
Mathurine GRATON	177	1670
Marie GRONDIN	182	1668
Marie Martine GRONIER	138	1669
Catherine GUERTIN	157 & 170	1673
Marie HUS	118 & 436	1667
Marie Charlotte JOLIVET	113 & 431	1671
Marie Marguerite JOURDAIN	159 & 183 & 482	1667
Marie Anne LAGUEUX	122	1670
Anne LAINÉ	117 & 434	1669
Charlotte LAMARCHE	175 & 497	1669
Marie LANGLOIS	175	1665
Francoise LATIER	129 & 453	1669
Catherine LAWLOR	180 & 506	1671
Marie LEBRUN	450	1667
Denise LECLERC	166 & 180 & 490	1669

Continued on next page...

TABLE 3 – *FILLES DU ROI* (continued)

Name	Chart	Arrived	Name	Chart	Arrived
Marie Marthe LEFEBVRE	187 & 514	1670	Jeanne PETIT	72	1672
Marie LELONG	89	1671	Marie Therese PETIT	79.1	1669
Marie LEMAIRE	105	1669	Nicole PHILIPPEAU	171	1671
Anne LEPERE	91	1673	Fancoise PILOY	128 & 452	1669
Marie LEROUX	105	1668	Marie Catherine PLAT	169	1663
Marguerite LEVAIGNEUR	480	1667	Marie Madeleine PLOUART	152	1667
Isabelle LOPS	85	1670	Marie Anne POUSSIN	79.3	1665
Marie Denise MARIER	76 & 125	1673	Marie RENAUD	181 & 508	1668
Marie MARTIN (b.1648)	151	1671	Marie Anne RICHARD	185	1669
Marie MARTIN (b.1649)	516	1665	Marguerite RICHER	95 & 227	1672
Anne Francoise MARTIN	517	1669	Marie Henriette ROUSSEAU	116	1668
Anne MASSON	103 & 176	1670	Charlotte ROUSSEL	100	1668
Louise MENACIER	94 & 413	1663	Jeanne SEDERAY	107 & 120	1669
Marie Anne METRU	94	1671	Marguerite TENARD	92 & 409	1665
Marguerite MOREAU	93	1670	Marguerite VAILLANT	155 & 477	1668
Marie Charlotte MORIN	178 & 500	1665	Marie VALADE	77	1663
Eleonore MOUILLARD	121	1671	Marie Pierrette VALLÉE	123 & 445	1665
Catherine PAULO	134	1663	Marie VARA	146	1671
Marie Marthe PAYANT	109	1670	Marie Therese VIEL	101	1671

SOLDIERS 1665-1783

A number of early settlers in New France were soldiers. Prior to 1665, a small number of *engagés* had been hired in France specifically to act as armed guards around Quebec City, Trois-Rivières and Montreal to defend the *Canadiens* from the constant attacks by the Iroquois. Some of these men would later form the core of local militia companies which were eventually established and which enlisted all able-bodied males between the ages of 16 and 60.[Eccles, "Military Establishment", p.3]

After New France was declared a Royal colony in 1663, an attempt was made to impose a lasting peace with the Iroquois by sending 1,200 regular troops of the French Army to Canada. More than 1,000 of these troops came with the Carignan-Salières Regiment. The regiment had been formed in France in 1658. A typical French infantry regiment, it was made up of 20 companies of 50 soldiers each, plus officers. The first ancestor to arrive in Canada bearing the Seguin name, Francois SEGUIN *dit* Laderoute, was likely a soldier in Captain Saint-Ours' company of the Carignan-Salières Regiment. Francois may have been with the regiment while it was in garrison for several years at Marsal in the province of Lorraine in the east of France [Robert-Lionel Seguin, p.22], or he could have been recruited as the regiment marched across the country to their embarkation point at La Rochelle in early 1665. (See also *Appendix B – Francois Seguin's Arrival in Canada.*)

Arriving on the French coast in April of that year, the regiment was confined to the islands of Oléron and Ré, just offshore from La Rochelle. This was partly to keep the often raucous soldiers separate from the civilian population, but also to prevent the desertion of any recruits who might be having second thoughts about being sent to the wilds of North America. While waiting for the six ships that would be needed to transport them and their supplies across the Atlantic Ocean, the soldiers were trained on the use of the army's new firearm, the flintlock musket. At that time, most of the French Army was still armed with the matchlock arquebus, a heavy, long-barrelled firearm which used a length of burning wick attached to a spring-loaded lever which would ignite the gunpowder when the trigger was pulled. The flintlock musket was a much more reliable weapon and it had a higher rate of fire as it used a flint (instead of a wick) which, when the trigger was pulled, would strike a steel frizzen to create sparks to ignite the gunpowder to discharge the weapon.

The first four companies of the Carignan-Salières Regiment boarded the ship, *Le Saint Siméon*, and left for New France in April, 1665. [Verney refers to this ship as *Le Joyeux Siméon*] They arrived at Quebec City two months later. The Saint-Ours company was one of the last to leave La Rochelle. The soldiers of the company boarded the ship, *La Justice*, on May 24, 1665, along with three other companies of the regiment. Over the course of the next three months, the ship's captain, Pierre Guillet, needed all of his considerable skill and experience to navigate through rough seas with adverse winds and numerous storms. It took the ship almost sixteen weeks to cross the Atlantic Ocean and make its way up the St. Lawrence River. The soldiers finally disembarked at Quebec City on September 14. Eight men had died during the passage and many more had become very sick as a result of inadequate nutrition and poor sanitary conditions aboard *La Justice*. The sick were carried off the ship; some to Quebec's Hôtel-Dieu hospital, but it quickly ran out of beds, so the others were taken to the nearby church and convent to be cared for by the Ursuline nuns. After many days in hospital, most of the patients were fit enough to be discharged, however as many as thirty-five died, likely from the effects of scurvy contracted during the Atlantic crossing. [Fournier & Langlois, pp. 12, 26, 34]

The new military commander of New France, Lieutenant-General Alexandre de Prouville Marquis de Tracy, had already arrived in New France with 200 soldiers from a mixed contingent of troops from companies of the Allier, Chambellé, Orléans and Poitou regiments who had just defeated the Dutch in the West Indies. These four companies which accompanied Tracy brought the total number of French regulars in New France to more than 1,200.

The first task assigned to the newly arrived soldiers was the construction of a series of forts that could be used as bases from which to launch attacks into Iroquois territory. In October, 1665, Captain Saint-Ours was ordered to take his company of the Carignan-Salières Regiment to join others already working along the Richelieu River building Fort St. Louis (later called Fort Chambly). Before the year was out, the company was sent down the Richelieu to where it joined the St. Lawrence River. Here, Captain Saurel's company had rebuilt the old post of Fort Richelieu (at present-day Sorel, Que.) where both companies spent their first winter in Canada.

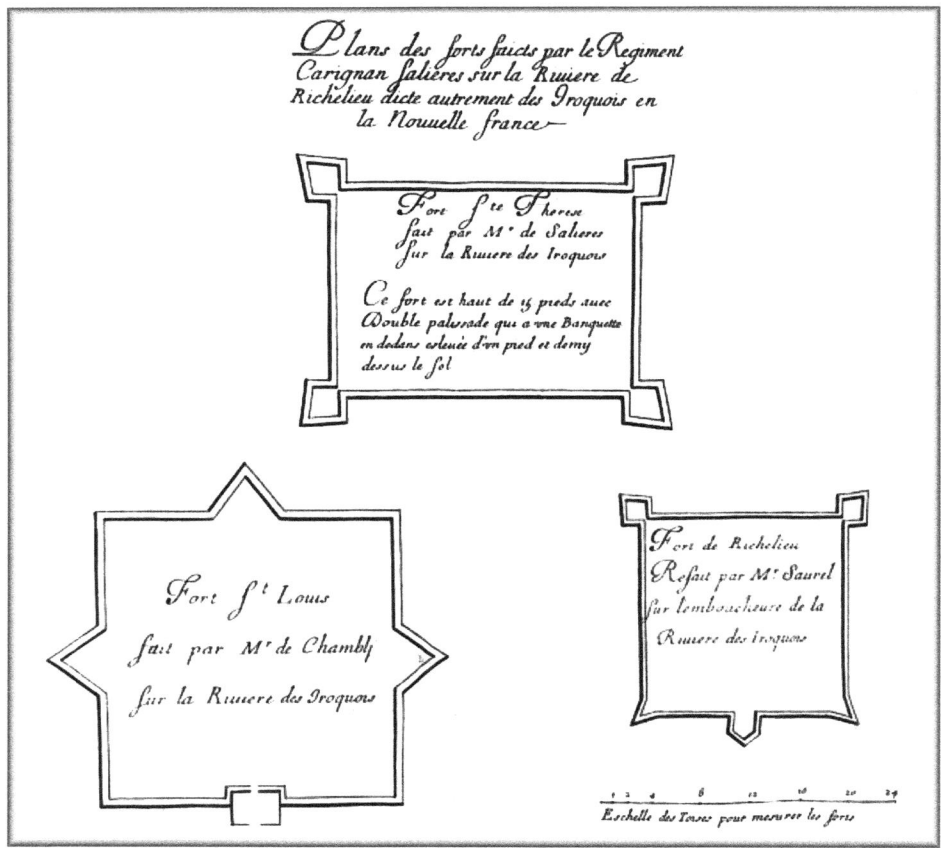

Three of the Richelieu River forts constructed by the Carignan-Salières Regiment, 1665.
[Detail from the map by Francois Lemercier. Library & Archives Canada, NMC6383.]

In December, 1665, four tribes of the Five Nations Confederacy; the Senecas, Onondagas, Oneidas and Cayugas, entered into peace negotiations with the French. The Mohawks, whose territory was closest to the French settlements, refused to join in the talks. The Marquis de Tracy and the governor of New France, Daniel Rémy de Courcelles, feared that the Mohawks would continue attacks on French colonists and their Indigenous allies and further interrupt the French fur-trade. On January 9, 1666, Courcelles, set out on a poorly prepared military expedition against the Mohawks. Some 240 French regulars, unaccustomed to the use of snowshoes, along with 200 colonial volunteers and a number of their Indigenous allies converged at Fort St. Louis on the Richelieu River. From there, they marched for weeks through deep snow.

After losing several men from sickness and exposure, they finally engaged in a skirmish with a war party of forty Mohawks near Schenectady, New York, on February 20. During the brief battle, at least six men of the French force were killed. The expedition then quickly retreated back to Canada; the last survivors arriving back at the French settlements at the end of March.

The ill-conceived winter campaign had been a disaster for the French. Courcelles, having arrived in North America for the first time in the summer of 1665, had little understanding of the difficulties in mounting a military expedition in the middle of a Canadian winter. Total French casualties vary depending on the sources consulted — something between 60 and 400 men died, became sick or were wounded. [See Verney and Fournier & Langlois]

Carignan-Salières Regiment, winter campaign uniform, 1666.

[L. Rousselot, plate 1, from Albert Dépréaux, *Les Uniformes des Troupes Coloniales de 1666 à 1875,* Paris, 1931. Bibliotheque Nationale de France, ark:12148.]

After further peace negotiations with the Mohawks failed that summer, the Marquis de Tracy launched another military campaign in the autumn of 1666. This force was composed of 600 French Army regulars (including the Saint-Ours company), 600 militia and 100 Indigenous allies. [www.biographi.ca /en/bio/saint_ours_pierre_de _2E.html] Their primary objective was to finally secure a decisive military victory over the Mohawks. Secondarily, Tracy planned to attack the former Dutch settlements, now in English hands, at Schenectady and Albany (Fort Orange) as France was an ally of Holland in the Anglo-Dutch War which had started the year before.

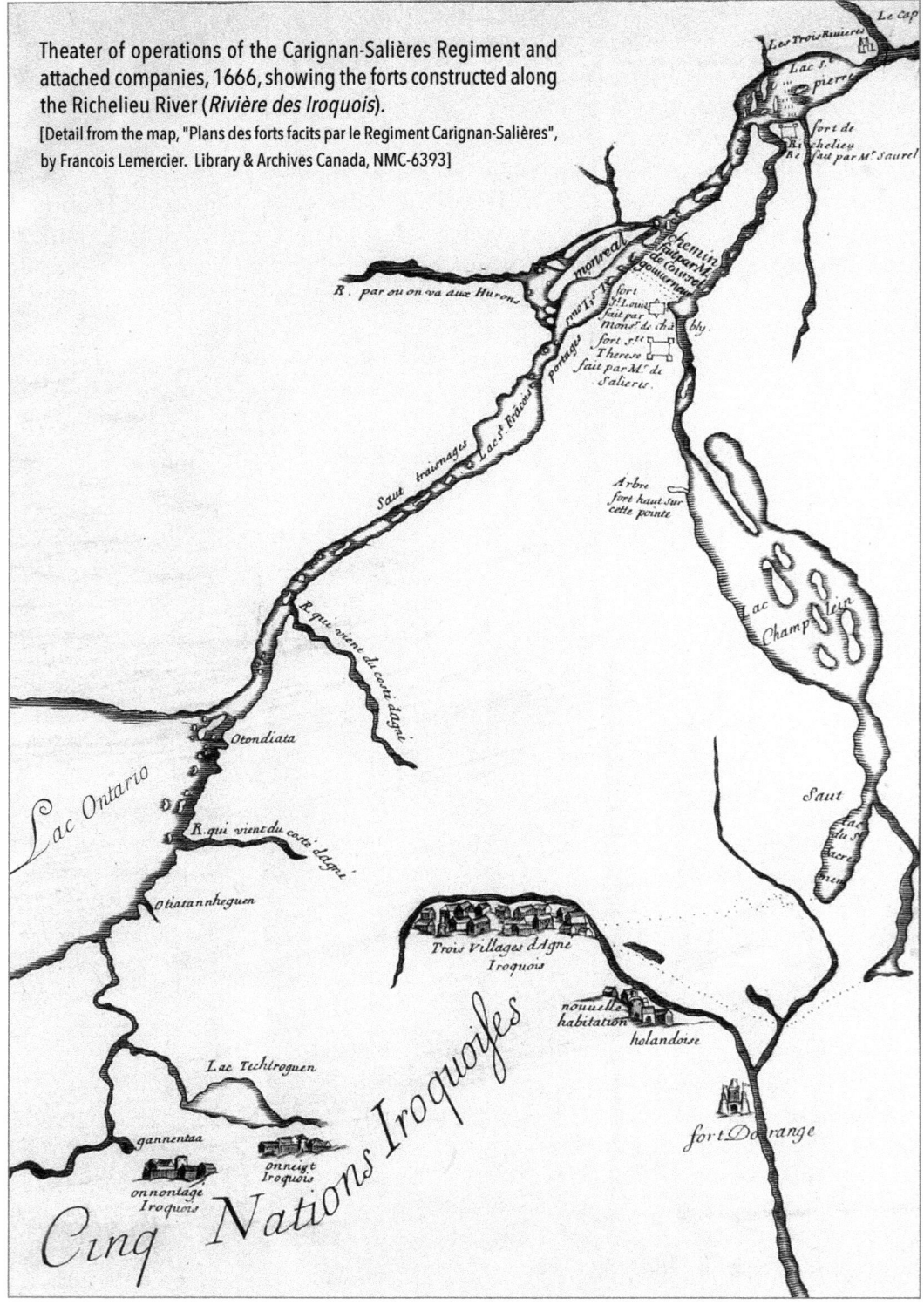

Theater of operations of the Carignan-Salières Regiment and attached companies, 1666, showing the forts constructed along the Richelieu River (*Rivière des Iroquois*).
[Detail from the map, "Plans des forts facits par le Regiment Carignan-Salières", by Francois Lemercier. Library & Archives Canada, NMC-6393]

Tracy's army gathered at Fort Chambly and then travelled up the Richelieu River, crossed Lake Champlain and Lake George, and ventured deep into Mohawk territory where they burned four Iroquois villages which had been abandoned on the approach of the French forces. Although he did not engage in battle with the Mohawks and he did not attack the English settlements, Tracy declared a victory and returned to Quebec City.

In 1667, all of the tribes of the Five Nations Confederacy agreed to peace terms with the French. The Carignan-Salières regiment had accomplished its primary mission, and soon each company of the regiment began returning to France. By the end of 1668, the bulk of the French regulars had left Canada. However, more than 400 of these troops, including some of the officers, chose to settle in the colony. Most of these soldiers married and raised families in New France. Of those, forty-four have been identified as ancestors of Theodore Seguin or Alphonsine Seguin. (see page 34) This includes Francois SEGUIN *dit* Laderoute (Ch.72-2), a 5th-great-grandfather of both Theodore and Alphonsine. (see *Appendix A-1*)

As one of the few officers of the Carignan-Salières Regiment who chose to settle in Canada, Pierre de Saint-Ours was eventually granted a large tract of land in the colony. Some 9,000 acres of forest — bordered on one side by the south shore of the St. Lawrence River and on another side by the Richelieu River — became the Saint-Ours seigneury over which Pierre de Saint-Ours held domain as seigneur. Thirty-one soldiers and two officers in his company also chose to remain in New France. The officers would be granted seigneuries of their own. The soldiers were granted a bonus of 100 *livres* (about CDN$2,000 in 2023) along with uncleared land on the Saint-Ours seigneury. Francois SEGUIN was among the settlers on Captain Saint-Ours' seigneury. The land he was given would have been typical of many of the seigneurial grants: long, narrow lots that averaged around three *arpents* (570 feet) of river frontage and thirty *arpents* (5700 feet) in depth [Eccles, Canada, p.49], an area of approximately seventy-five acres. Direct access to a waterway was vital for transportation at a time when roads were non-existant. The resulting "ribbon farms" along rivers were a common form of land division and settlement throughout much of New France.

Francois, it seems, had not been ready to settle down and start a new life as a farmer. In 1669, when a large group of ex-soldiers in France was recruited to help populate Canada and to reinforce the colony's militia companies [Eccles, "Military Establishment", p.3], Captain Saint-Ours was given command of the Montreal garrison. He recruited seventy-five of these new arrivals, along with Francois SEGUIN, to help defend Montreal in the event of further Iroquois attacks. (see also *Appendix B*)

TABLE 4 – ANCESTORS IN THE CARIGNAN-SALIÈRES REGIMENT AND ATTACHED COMPANIES

Name	Company	Chart
Louis BADAILLAC *dit* Laplante	Froment	180 & 506
André BADEL	Grandfontaine	173 & 495
Mathurin BANLIER *dit* Laperle	Saint-Ours	165
Pierre BARBARY *dit* Grandmaison	Contrecoeur	126 & 450
Louis BARITEAU *dit* Lamarche	Chambly	146
Jean BARREAU (b. C.1651)	*Monteil – Poitou Regt.*	90
André BARSA *dit* Lafleur	La Fredyère	128 & 452
Antoine BAZINET *dit* Tourblanche	La Motte	182
Jean BEAULNE *dit* Lafranchise	La Varenne	82
Nicolas BONIN *dit* St. Martin	Saint-Ours	184
Etienne BOYER *dit* Lafontaine (b. C.1650)	La Fouille	101
Etienne CONTENT *dit* Bury	*Monteil – Poitou Regt.*	117 & 434
Bernard DELPECHE *dit* Belair	La Fredyère/Salières	159 & 482
Claude DESJARDINS *dit* Charbonnier	Duprat-Deportes	84 & 128
René DUMAS *dit* Rencontre	Rougemont	89
Antoine EMERY *dit* Codère	Contrecoeur	184 & 188
Mathieu FAILLÉ *dit* Lafayette	La Varenne	93
Christophe FEVRIER *dit* Lacroix	La Fouille	151 & 173
Jacques GUITAUT *dit* Jolicoeur	Dugué	92 & 412
Jacques HENAULT *dit* Canada	Saurel	105
Jean LALONDE	*Monteil – Poitou Regt.*	106 & 427
Pierre LAMOUREUX *dit* St. Germain	La Fouille	101
Noel LAURENCE (b. C.1647)	La Fouille	159
Francois LEROUX *dit* Cardinal	La Fouille	181 & 508
Pierre LESIEGE *dit* Fontaine	Saurel	158
Jean LESPINAY de Bonbardot (lieutenant)	Rougemont	160
René MAILLOT *dit* Laviolette (b.1644)	Duprat-Deportes	187 & 515
Louis MAJEAU *dit* Maisonseule	La Fouille	183
Pierre MARSAN *dit* Lapierre (sergeant)	Chambly	78
Nicolas MOISON *dit* Parisien	La Fredyère	462
Leonard MONTREUIL *dit* Francoeur	Froment	480
Etienne PAQUET (b.1621)	La Motte	116
Isaac-Etienne PAQUET *dit* Lavallée	La Motte	189 & 519
Pierre PAYET *dit* St. Amour (b.1641)	La Motte/Latour	130 & 136
Jean-Baptiste PERRIER *dit* Lafleur	*La Bisardière – Orléans Regt.*	126 & 449
Pierre PERTHUIS *dit* Lalime (b.1645)	Salières	135
Francois PINSONNAULT *dit* Lafleur	Saint-Ours	91
Pierre RICHER *dit* Laflêche	Grandfontaine	180 & 507
Louis ROBERT *dit* Lafontaine	Laubia	137 & 461
René SAUVAGEAU *dit* Maisonneuve (surgeon)	Dugué	142
Francois SEGUIN *dit* Laderoute	**Saint-Ours**	**72**
Pierre TABEAU *dit* Le Petit Leveille (b.1645)	Contrecoeur	113 & 432
Pierre TOUPIN	*La Bisardière – Orléans Regt.*	177
Jacques VIAU *dit* Lesperance	Dugué	152

By 1672, at age 28, Francois had ended his military career. He sold his partially-cleared land on the Saint-Ours seigneury and leased a small lot and a house just across the river from Montreal, at Boucherville, Que., in the seigneury of Pierre Boucher. On September 21, 1672, Francois signed a marriage contract with 16-year-old Jeanne PETIT, a newly-arrived *fille du Roi*. The following day, he purchased a 50-*arpent* lot which included a shed and a few acres of cleared land along with a barn and a house under construction. Presumably the house was completed in time for their wedding on October 31. The following April, the seigneur granted Francois a 100-*arpent* lot fronting on the St. Lawrence River just two kilometers south of the village centre. There, he took up farming and worked as a weaver. He and Jeanne raised eight children at Boucherville — three daughters and five sons.* Francois died in 1704. Jeanne, supported by her children, lived at Lachenaie, Que., then at Longueuil until her death in 1733. [Gareau, pp.12, 66. Seguin-Pharand, pp.10-18]

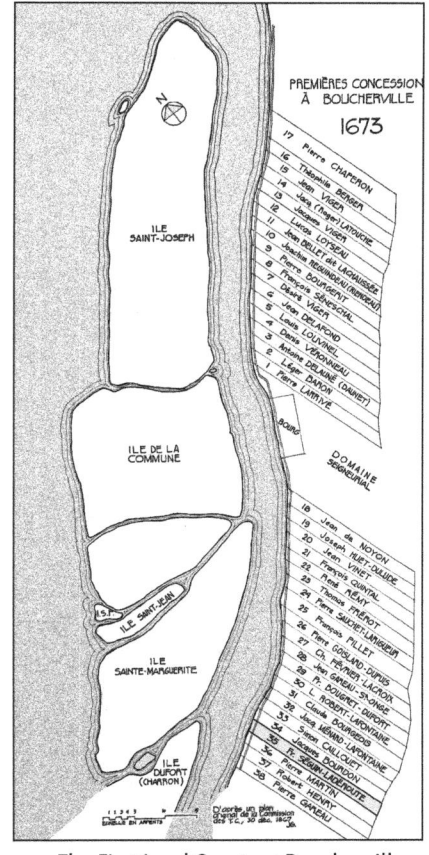

The First Land Grants at Boucherville, 1673. [Gareau, Georges R. *Boucherville*, p.13.]

Nine Seguin ancestors were among the early recipients of farm lots on the seigneury of Pierre Boucher:

- Jacques BOURDON (Lot 34)
- Jean-Baptiste DENOYON (Lot 18)
- Christophe FEVRIER
  dit Lacroix (Lot 27) †
- Pierre GAREAU (Lot 38)
- Lucas LOISEAU (Lot 12)
- Jacques MENARD
  dit Lafontaine (Lot 32) †
- Louis ROBERT
  dit Lafontaine (Lot 30) †
- Francois SEGUIN
  dit Laderoute (Ch.72-2) †
- Denis VERONNEAU (Lot 4)

(† Ex-soldier in the Carignan-Salières Regiment)

Unfortunately, the peace with the Iroquois that had been secured by the presence of the French Army did not last. In an attempt to gain complete control of the fur-trade, the Five Nations Confederacy continued to come into conflict with the colonists of New France and their native allies. The Iroquois were encouraged by their new allies, the English, who had taken over the North American territories and fur-trading ambitions of the Dutch. The local militia companies at Quebec City, Trois-Rivières and Montreal, always under-strength, were insufficient to defend the colony

---

* Two daughters and one son died in infancy.

from the constant attacks on the settlements and disruption of the fur-trade. By 1683, in order to help protect the *Canadiens* and counter the increasing number of Iroquois raids, more regular soldiers from France were sent to North America. These soldiers, under the authority of the French government's Department of Marine and Colonies, served in the *Compagnies Franches de la Marine;* independent military companies of the Marine Department, also known as the *Troupes de la Marine.* These companies were stationed in the major population centres as well as at outlying missions and fur-trading posts all across France's North American possessions from Newfoundland to the Mississippi River. The *Troupes de la Marine* were employed largely in a defensive mode, but they did participate in sporadic offensive actions against Iroquois war parties as well as against American colonial militia during several minor European wars which spilled over into North America throughout the late 17th and early 18th centuries. During the Seven Years War in North America (the French and Indian War, 1755-1760), they also saw action against regular troops of the British Army in most of the major battles of that conflict.

While a number of soldiers in the *Troupes de la Marine* were recruited from the colonial population , as many as twenty percent of those who had come from France chose to remain in the colony and start families after their discharge from military service. [Dechêne, *Habitants*, p.41] More than forty of those soldiers who had arrived from France between 1684 and 1759 are ancestors of Theodore Seguin or Alphonsine Seguin.

Soldiers in the *Troupes de la Marine, 1695 and 1755*
(*Les Compagnies Franches de la Marine*)
[Detail of paintings by A. d'Auriac, 1932. Bibliotheque et Archives Nationale de Quebec. ID 327269 and ID 327268]

TABLE 5 – ANCESTORS IN THE *TROUPES DE LA MARINE*

Name	Company	Arrived	Chart
Abel Joseph BARBE (Joseph BEAR *dit* Barbe)	unknown	c.1695	84
Jean-Baptiste BARBEAU *dit* Boisdoré	Jadon de Cirgues (St. Cirque)	c.1686	73
Pierre BIROLEAU *dit* Lafleur (b. C.1670)	Greysolon Duluth	c.1692	78
Jacques BONNIER	Le Prévost de St. Jean	c.1685	96
Pierre BRAULT	Jordy de Cabanac	c.1695	158
Esprit CARBONNEAU *dit* Provençal	unknown	c.1670	125
Jean-Baptiste CHAPEAU *dit* Laframboise	Jousselin de Marigny	c.1710	189
Pierre CLEMENT *dit* Larivière	unknown	c.1702	127
Jean CORON	Crisafy-Grimaldi (after 1684)	c.1668	131
Francois DARAGON *dit* Lafrance	unknown	c.1695	156
Francois DARVEAU *dit* Langoumois	unknown	c.1690	117
Julien DELIÈRES	Lacorne de Chaptes	c.1708	156
Jean-Baptiste DESFORGES	Lorimier	c.1685	95
Jean-Baptiste DUFORT *dit* Lacouture	unknown	c.1759	15 & 112
Pierre DUMESNIL *dit* Lamusique	Le Gouès de Graye et de Merville	c.1690	149
Francois FRANCOEUR (sergeant)	Ramezay	c.1689	149
Jacques FROMENT	Le Fournier du Vivier	c.1688	167
Francois GEORGET *dit* Tranquille	Lacorne de Chaptes	c.1716	97
Louis GILBERT *dit* Comtois (b. C.1698)	Amariton	c.1720	181
Guillaume GOYAU *dit* Lagarde	Jadon de Cirgues (St. Cirque)	c.1685	155
Jacques GRIGNON	Rigaud de Vaudreuil	c.1690	180
Thomas HÉBERT	unknown	c.1670	145
Pierre JAMME *dit* Carrière	Le Gardeur de Repentigny (Croisille)	1687	126
Leonard LALANDE *dit* Latreille (sergeant)	Lorimier	c.1695	82
Jean-Baptiste LAVIGNE *dit* Brisetout	unknown	c.1699	152
Jean-Baptiste LEFORT *dit* Laforest	Tonty de Paludy	c.1705	150
Pierre MAISONNEUVE	Blaise des Bergères	c.1695	129
Jean-Baptiste MALBOEUF *dit* Beausoleil	unknown	c.1690	138
Jean-Baptiste MAROTTE	Monbeton de Bourrouillan	c.1689	144
Jean-Baptiste MARTIN	Le Ber de Senneville	c.1720	14 & 104
Hugues MESSAGUÉ *dit* Laplaine	Guillon de Cloches	c.1684	83 & 127
Jean MIGNERON *dit* Lajeunesse	Villiers ?	c.1684	159
Francois MOITIÉ *dit* Lafonderie (b. C.1706) (corporal)	Payan de Noyan	c.1740	20 & 148
Pierre MORIN (sergeant)	unknown	c.1690	160
Joseph POIRIER *dit* Desloge	Lacorne de Chaptes	c.1705	100
Hubert RANGER	Lorimier	c.1684	113
Mathieu RINGUETTE *dit* Laplante	Monbeton de Bourrouillan	c.1685	178
Bernard RUFIANGE *dit* Laviolette	unknown	c.1695	89
Jacques SEGUIN*	unknown	c.1685	173
Jacques VALLERAND (b. C.1686)	Marquis de la Groye d'Aloigny	c.1710	96
Raymond VEGIARD *dit* Labonté	Le Fournier du Vivier	c.1688	169
Thomas WATIER *dit* Lanois	Migeon de la Gauchetiere	c.1735	114

* No connection has been found between Jacques Seguin from Limoges, France, and Francois Seguin from Picardie, France.

In 1755, when war between France and Great Britain broke out in North America (the precursor to the Seven Years War in Europe), regular troops of the French Army were sent to New France to reinforce the *Troupes de la Marine*. The first two of ten regiments to arrive in the colony over the next three years were the Languedoc Regiment and the Béarn Regiment, both of which arrived at Quebec City in June, 1755. Among the soldiers of these regiments were Pierre COGNAC *dit* Léveillé and Jacques NOUVION, both Seguin ancestors who eventually settled in Canada.*

Pierre COGNAC *dit* Léveillé (Ch.20-6), a 3rd-great-grandfather of Alphonsine Seguin (on her father's side) was a soldier in Captain Douglas' company of the Languedoc Regiment. He was 32 years old when he left France in 1755 and, by then, he had likely served in the French Army for some time. As soon as the regiment arrived in North America, an expeditionary force including 200 French regulars along with Canadian militia and Nipissing and Wabanaki warriors was dispatched up the Richelieu River and across Lake Champlain to Fort St. Frédéric (Crown Point, NY). There, in September, 1755, they were repulsed by Iroquois warriors and American colonial militia at the Battle of Lake George. The Languedoc Regiment was then sent to Fort Carillon (Ticonderoga, NY). It appears that Pierre COGNAC, with a detachment of the regiment, was sent back to the Richelieu River post of Fort Chambly. That is where Pierre married Marie Josephte LEFORT in February, 1757.

In August of that year, as part of a force of 8,000 French regulars, militia and Indigenous North American allies under the command of General Louis-Joseph Marquis de Montcalm, the regiment took part in the siege of Fort William Henry, the British-held fort on Lake George. After the British surrendered, many who left the fort under a flag of truce were massacred by the native allies of the French. The following year, the 2nd Battalion, Languedoc Regiment, was involved in a major victory over the British at the Battle of Carillon (Fort Ticonderoga) when a French army of 3,600 defeated a force of more than 18,000, including 6,000 British regulars.

Soldier in the French Army of the mid-18th Century.
[Denis Diderot, *Receuil de Planches....* Paris, 1763.]

---

* There was also a Captain Seguin commanding a company of the Béarn Regiment. [Tanguay, *A Travers le Régistres*. p.177]. While this officer did not settle in Canada after the war, further research might find a connection between him and the other Seguin ancestors of Theodore and Alphonsine.

By 1759, the regiment was back in Quebec City, defending the town against the advancing British. During the British siege of Quebec, the Languedoc regiment took part in the Battle at Montmorency. Then, on September 13, under the command of the Marquis de Montcalm, the regiment, along with the Béarn Regiment, held the centre of the French line of battle as they formed up on the farm that once belonged to the Seguin ancestor, Abraham MARTIN *dit* L'Écossais (Ch.456) (see *Appendix A-10*). There they faced the British Army under the command of General James Wolfe. The Battle of the Plains of Abraham resulted in a British victory, and the Languedoc Regiment, together with the remainder of the defeated French Army, withdrew to Montreal.

The following spring, the French launched a counter-attack and met the British just west of Quebec City at Ste. Foy. The Battle of Ste. Foy in 1760 was the last major battle of the Seven Years War in North America. The French Army was defeated and the governor of New France, Pierre de Rigaud Marquis de Vaudreuil, capitulated to the British. By the Treaty of Paris three years later, France ceded Canada to Great Britain.

Jacques NOUVION (Ch.21-4), another of Alphonsine Seguin's 3rd-great-grandfathers (on her father's side) also arrived in Canada in June, 1755. At age 19, he was likely a new recruit in Captain Jourdeau's company of the Béarn Regiment. The regiment was sent to Fort Frontenac (Kingston, Ont.) in July, 1755. In August of the following year, they participated in the capture of Fort Oswego, the British stronghold on Lake Ontario. The regiment was at the Battle of Carillon in 1758, and participated in the Battle of the Plains of Abraham at Quebec City in September, 1759. After the French defeat, the regiment spent the winter in Montreal, then formed part of the counter-attack expedition in April, 1760, when they fought in the Battle of Ste. Foy. In October, 1760, shortly after New France capitulated to the British, Jacques NOUVION married Marie Anne LAVIGNE (Ch.21-5) at Varennes, Que, just downstream from Montreal on the south shore of the St. Lawrence River.

The last direct Seguin ancestor known to arrive in North America from Europe was also a soldier. In 1777, during the American War of Independence, Gebhardt NIEDING (Ch.13-6) from town of Gelnhaar (north-east of Frankfurt), in the German state of Hesse-Hanau, was one of the so-called "Hessian mercenaries" who was sent to North America to support the British Army in its fight against the American rebels. The British government had contracted with several German states to provide as many as 30,000 troops for the North American conflict. These included artillery, cavalry and infantry soldiers. In addition, several elite rifle regiments formed part of the German contingent. One of these regiments was Karl Adolph von Kreuzbourg's Jaeger Corps, which had recruited the 23-year-old Gebhardt NIEDING for service with British troops in North America. He was one of Theodore Seguin's 3rd-great-grandfathers (on his father's side) (see *Appendix A-12*).

Like all 400 volunteers in the Corps, Gebhardt was likely recruited because of his hunting skills and his experience using a rifle, a firearm with greater accuracy and a longer range than the standard-issue smoothbore infantry musket. Von Kreuzbourg's jaegers were deployed as skirmishers and used their rifles with great effect in 1777 at the Battle of Oriskany and at the siege of Fort Stanwix. Afterwards, they were in garrison at Quebec City, Montreal and La Prairie, Que.

When the Corps was disbanded after the war, in July 1783, many of its soldiers, along with those of other German regiments, settled in Canada. Gebhardt NIEDING was one of these settlers. Three years later, he married Marie Angelique GAGNÉ (Ch.13-7) at La Prairie, Que., where they raised eight children.

Soldier in Von Kreuzbourg's Jaeger Corps, 1777
[Artist unknown. Hessian State Archives.
Courtesy of Kim Kujawski www.tfcg.ca]

Since 1777, no more Seguin ancestors have arrived in North America from Europe. However, some English colonists who had originally immigrated to Britain's American colonies, and from whom Theodore and Alphonsine are descended, had been taken to Canada against their will as part of the long-running conflicts between European colonists and Indigenous North Americans.

✑ ✑ ✑ ✑

Colonists vs. Natives

Armed conflicts between Indigenous North American peoples and European colonists were often a by-product of commercial trading rivalries between European nations who frequently used their native allies as proxies in the fight to control the North American fur-trade. First the Dutch and then, after 1664, the English who colonized much of the eastern seaboard from Maine to the Carolinas, allied themselves with the Iroquois Confederacy (Haudenosaunee) whose traditional homeland extended through present-day upstate New York from the Hudson River westward along the Mohawk Valley to the Finger Lakes district south of Lake Ontario. The French, whose principal settlements in the 17th Century were along the St. Lawrence River at Quebec City, Trois-Rivières and Montreal, allied themselves with Indigenous North American peoples in present-day, Quebec, Ontario, Michigan, Wisconsin and Illinois: the Montagnais, Wabanaki, Anishinaabe and Wendat. As French fur-traders moved ever westward in their search for more and more beaver skins, they also formed alliances with many of the Algonkian- and Siouan-speaking peoples of the western Great Lakes region and beyond.

While inter-tribal warfare had been part of the culture of many Indigenous North America peoples for centuries, the European presence in North America exacerbated this situation. As early as 1609, in an attempt to stop Iroquois incursions into the traditional fur trapping territory of the Wabanaki and Algonquin peoples, Samuel de Champlain had organized an expedition of French volunteers and Indigenous allies to attack the Mohawk who lived near Lake Champlain. This successful raid was followed by a failed attempt to destroy an Onondaga village south of Lake Ontario in 1615.

These actions hardened the Five Nations against the French and their allies. In addition, the Iroquois continued to followed their customary practice of replacing their fallen warriors with enemy captives who would be adopted into Iroquois clans if they were not first enslaved, tortured to death or killed outright. Other native peoples had similar customs. This resulted in a never-ending cycle of "mourning wars" — reprisal after reprisal during which captives were taken. In this manner, by 1649, the Iroquois had virtually exterminated the Wendat. As the 17th Century progressed and the Iroquois ventured further and further north and west to trap beaver, violent encounters with other Indigenous nations and their French allies became more frequent.

It was into this environment of ongoing Indigenous inter-tribal warfare and deadly commercial rivalries among Europeans that colonists from France, Britain and elsewhere tried to establish permanent settlements in North America in the 17th and early 18th centuries.

Champlain and His Indigenous Allies Attacking the Iroquois, 1609.
["Deffaite des Yroquois a Lac de Champlain" from *Les Voyages de Sieur de Champlain*,
Paris, 1613. Cornell University Library]

After the Carignan-Salières Regiment arrived and military expeditions against the Iroquois were mounted, an uneasy peace was achieved. Throughout the late 17th and into the 18th Century, intermittent periods of peace were interspersed with periods of warfare which saw the military forces of New France — the *Troupes de la Marine*, the militia and their native allies — launching attacks and counter-attacks against Iroquois villages and English settlements in the American colonies. These were met with reprisals against French settlements.

In response to the expeditions led by New France's governor, Marquis de Denonville, against the Seneca in 1686 and 1687, the Mohawks, encouraged by their English allies during the course of the Nine Years War (also known as King William's War, 1688-1697), launched one of the most devastating assaults on Montreal Island. In the early morning hours of August 5, 1689, some 1,500 Mohawk warriors attacked the French settlement of Lachine. Most of the houses and barns were burned to the ground and as many as 240 of the 375 inhabitants were killed, including four of the ancestors of Theodore Seguin and Alphonsine Seguin. This became known as the "Lachine Massacre". Several French settlers were taken captive during the raid; all of who were tortured to death or enslaved or, if able-bodied children, adopted into Iroquois clans.

Between 1648 and 1709, at least fourteen Seguin ancestors in New France were killed by the Iroquois during their raids on French settlements. In addition, at least nine others were captured by the Iroquois but later escaped, were ransomed back to the French or were exchanged for other prisoners that had been taken by New France's native allies.

TABLE 6 – ANCESTORS KILLED OR CAPTURED BY IROQUOIS

NAME	LOCATION	YEAR	NOTE	CHART
Pierre LEFEBVRE	Trois Rivières, Que.	1648	Captured, later escaped.	108
Leonard LUCOS	Point St. Charles, Montreal	1651	Killed	109
Michel MESSIER	Ville Marie (Montreal)	1652	Captured, exchanged 1655. Captured again, 1661, escaped 1663.	15
Pierre GARMAN	Trois Rivières, Que.	1653	Captured along with his son, Charles. Pierre was killed C.1653, Charles was adopted by the Oneida.	174
Julien GAGNÉ	Ville Marie (Montreal)	1655	Killed	98
Louis GAGNÉ	Beaupré, Que.	1661	Captured and killed.	132
Marin JANOT	Montreal	1661	Captured, escaped or ransomed.	182
Urbain TESSIER	Montreal	1661	Captured, exchanged 1662.	130
René CUILLERIER	Montreal	1661	Captured, tortured, adopted, then escaped ,1663.	10
André CYR	Ile Jesus, Que.	1689	Killed	131
Marie Madeleine BARBARY	Lachine, Que.	1689	Captured with her parents and three siblings. Later released with 1 sibling, 2 other adopted.	126
Marie LEBRUN	Lachine, Que.	1689	Captured and killed.	126
Pierre BARBARY	Lachine, Que.	1689	Captured and killed.	126
Marie CHANCY	Lachine, Que.	1689	Captured, killed.	127
Michel PRESSEAU	Lachine, Que.	1689	Captured, killed.	127
Julien GRENIER	Lachenaie, Que.	1689	Captured, killed.	44
René SAUVAGEAU	Lachenaie, Que.	1689	Killed – 5 of his 6 children were killed or captured along with his mother-in-law and sister-in-law.	142
Suzanne BETFER	Lachenaie, Que.	1689	Killed or captured along with 5 of her grand-children and one of her daughters.	142
Pierre PAYET	Rivière des Prairies, Que.	1690	Captured, tortured, enslaved, escaped 1693.	130
Marguerite MOREAU	La Prairie, Que.	1690	Captured and later ransomed or escaped.	93
Mathieu FAILLÉ	La Prairie, Que.	1690	Captured and later ransomed or escaped.	93
Hélène DODIN	Boucherville, Que	1695	Killed	88
Jean DAIGNEAU	Boucherville, Que	1695	Killed	88
Jean CADIEUX	Grand Calumet, Que.	1709	Killed	77

However, it was not only the Iroquois who engaged in the practice of capturing and killing their enemies. There is no doubt that Seguin ancestors killed at least as many Iroquois warriors in battle as were killed by them. Also, encouraged by their French allies, many Algonquins, Wabanakis and what were left of the Wendats engaged in raids on Iroquois and English settlements where they took prisoners and killed many people.

In September, 1677, in the aftermath of King Philip's War — a two year conflict in New England between native tribes and American colonists — a war party of Wabanakis attacked the remote settlement of Hatfield, Massachusetts. They killed thirteen inhabitants and took seventeen captives, mostly women and children, back to Sorel, Que. Two of the women were pregnant at the time of their capture and they both survived the gruelling 450 kilometer march to Canada. Stephen Jennings and Benjamin Waite, the husbands of these pregnant women, immediately set out to retrieve their wives, but they were forcibly stopped by the colonial authorities at Albany, New York, who believed the venture to be too hazardous and quite hopeless. Once the winter passed, the men again set out to find their wives. In the meantime, both women had given birth to baby girls that they named Captivity Jennings and Canada Waite. When the men finally reached Sorel in May, 1678, they found their wives and, with the intervention of the Comte de Frontenac, the governor of New France, they were able to pay a ransom of £200 for their release. Canada Waite is a 7th-great-grandmother of Marjorie Cluett, the wife of the author of this book. Sadly, Canada Waite's father and rescuer, Benjamin Waite, would be killed sixteen years later by a French and Indigenous force which raided the settlement of Deerfield, Massachusetts in 1704. [Creecy, pp.9-10]

In his book, *De la Nouvelle-Angleterre à la Nouvelle-France*, Marcel Fournier documents no fewer than 254 individual New Englanders who were captured by Indigenous war parties and brought to Canada in the late 17th Century and early 18th Century. Of those, less than half were ransomed back to their families or escaped their captors. The remainder either died in New France before they could return to New England, or they were adopted into Indigenous families, or they were ransomed by French families and integrated into *Canadien* society.

Several raids by French soldiers and their native allies on Puritan settlements in New England during the Nine Years' War (King William's War, 1688-1697) resulted in many captives being taken to Canada. In September, 1689, a war party raided the settlement at Cocheco in eastern New Hampshire (now Dover, NH). Twenty-three settlers were killed by the raiders and twenty-nine were captured and taken to Trois-Rivières, Que. Among the captives was 6-year-old Abigail Cursinwhitt. Abigail was soon adopted by a French family and baptised into the Roman Catholic faith as Louise Cosmouette. She remained in Canada and, in 1701, she became the first wife of Nicolas GLADU (Ch.175-2), with whom she had a son, Pierre, before she died giving birth to her second child in 1704. Nicolas then married Marie Louise LAPORTE (Ch.175-3). Abigail's son, Pierre, was a distant half-cousin of Alphonsine Seguin. [Fournier, p.118]

In January, 1692, a raiding party of Wabanaki warriors, Christianized Mohawk warriors (so-called "Praying Indians", allied with the French) and French soldiers descended on the settlement of York, Maine. Some 100 settlers were killed and 80 taken captive to the Sault St. Louis mission on Montreal's south shore (now the Kahnawake Reserve). Ten-year-old Hannah Heard was among the captives. Hannah, who was from Cocheco and likely knew Abigail Cursinwhitt, was twenty kilometers away in York, maybe visiting with her grandparents, John Heard and Elizabeth Hull, when the raid occurred. After enduring the gruelling mid-winter march to Sault St. Louis, Hannah was ransomed by Pierre Prudhomme, a master armourer at Montreal. She was one of only 10 captives of that raid who were not ransomed back to New England. Prudhomme employed Hannah in his home as a servant. In 1694, at age 13, she was baptised as "Marie Anne Herd" and confirmed into the Roman Catholic faith. In 1705 she married Sébastien Cholet *dit* Laviolette and together they had eleven children. Hannah Heard is a 7th-great-grandmother of the author's mother Loretta Ouellette. Also, since Hanna's grandparents are likely 10th-great-grandparents of the author's wife, Marjorie Cluett, the author and his wife are probably 11th-cousins.* (see *Appendix A-13*)

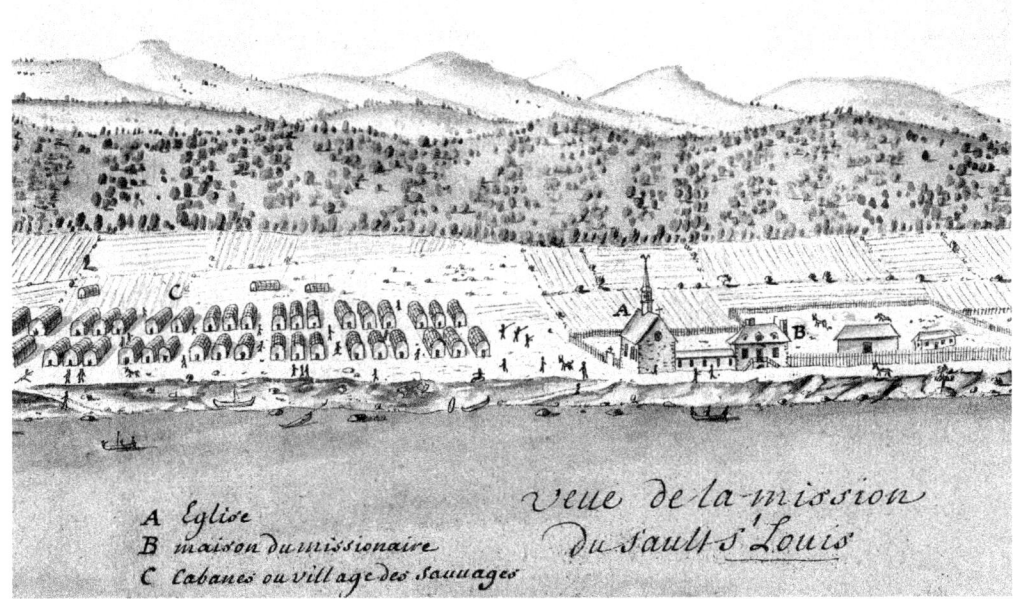

View of the Sault St. Louis Mission (detail), C.1675.
This is the Indigenous settlement near Montreal to where many New England captives were taken.
[Bibliotheque Nationale de France, ark:/12148/ btv1b52519254c]

---

* Sources: Marcel Fournier, *De la Nouvelle-Angleterre à la Nouvelle France*, p. 142.
   Cyprien Tanguay, *Dictionnaire Généalogique des Familles Canadiennes*, v.1, p.9.
   www.prdh-igd.com/Membership/en/PRDH/famille/9661.
   www.wikitree.com/wiki/Heard-171.
   https://en.wikipedia.org/wiki/Raid_on_York_(1692).
   https://newenglandhistoricalsociety.com/candlemas-massacre-salem-witch-trials/.

Several years later, in the North American theatre of the War of the Spanish Succession (Queen Anne's War, 1702-1713) a force of French militia and their native allies launched a winter attack on Deerfield, Massachusetts, in February, 1704. The "Deerfield Raid" resulted in the deaths of forty-seven English colonists and the capture of more than 100. The captives were force-marched 400 kilometers through the snow to the Sault St. Louis mission where some of the survivors were ransomed back to their families.

One of the captives, 11-year Sarah ALLEN, was never ransomed; instead, she was sold into servitude to a nearby *Canadien* merchant, Jean Quenet, who employed her as a domestic servant at Baie d'Urfé, Que. The next year, Sarah renounced her Protestant Puritanism and was baptised into the Roman Catholic faith as Marie Madeleine HÉLÈNE (Ch.106-3). In 1710, she married Guillaume LALONDE at Ste. Anne de Bellevue, Que. [Fournier, p.102]   Sarah ALLEN (Marie Madeleine HÉLÈNE) was a 5th-great-grandmother of Theodore Seguin (on his mother's side) (see *Appendix A-14*).

Between 1703 and 1712, the French and their Indigenous allies were involved in numerous raids, skirmishes and ambushes all across New England. One study has estimated that during this 10-year period, there were at least sixty-nine separate raids which saw some 392 English colonists captured. Of these, 243 survived — they were either ransomed back to their families, escaped captivity, stayed with their captors or were sold to the French. The remaining 149 individuals either died in captivity or their fate is unknown. [Haefeli & Sweeney, p.291]   No similar studies have been found which show the corresponding numbers of French colonists who were killed or captured by the Iroquois, or the numbers of Indigenous North Americans killed or captured by European soldiers and colonists.

While deadly conflicts between European settlers in Canada and Indigenous North Americans would continue long after the capitulation of New France to British forces in 1760 — from Pontiac's War in 1763 to the North West Rebellion in 1885 — further research is required to determine whether or not any Seguin ancestors were involved in these violent interactions.

Villains and Victims in New France

No family is perfect, and the Seguin family tree certainly has a few crooked branches and shady leaves of its own. Jeanne DEVOISY (Ch.174-13), a 7th-great-grandmother of Alphonsine Seguin (on her mother's side), was among these. Sometime after Jeanne arrived in New France with her husband and two sons in 1636, she was convicted and fined for selling alcohol to Indigenous North Americans living in the area of Sorel, Que.

In 1638, Nicolas MARSOLET *dit* St. Agnan (Ch.484-6), was again being accused of being a traitor (see page 22). His accuser was an enslaved African boy, Olivier Le Jeune, the slave/servant of Guillaume COUILLARD (Ch.485-6). Couillard was an 8th-great-grandfather of Alphonsine Seguin (on her mother's side). The enslaved boy had been brought to New France by the Kirke brothers in 1629 and sold to a man named Le Bailiff who had remained in the colony to work alongside the English invaders. This boy was the first known Black slave in New France. When the English, along with Le Baillif, left Quebec City in 1632, the boy was given to Guillaume COUILLARD. Couillard had him baptized with the name Olivier after sending him to school to learn how to read and write. Olivier's accusation, in 1638, that Marsolet had ongoing contact with the traitor Le Baillif was uncorroborated, so the African was found guilty of slander and sentenced to be clapped in irons for twenty-four hours and ordered to make a public apology to Marsolet. It is not known if Olivier Le Jeune was still in bondage when he died in 1654, or if Guillaume COUILLARD had granted him his freedom. [Trudel, pp. 15-17]

In 1647, a 7th-great-grandfather of Alphonsine's, Michel CHAUVIN (Ch.161-14) married Anne ARCHAMBAULT (Ch.161-15). In 1651, after fathering two children with Anne, the court at Quebec City was told that Michel already had a wife in France. His marriage to Anne was annulled and Michel CHAUVIN was charged with bigamy, but he fled back to France before he could be sentenced by the court. [PRDH]

These, however, were not the most serious offences committed by a Seguin ancestor.

A Swiss immigrant ancestor, Pierre MIVILLE *dit* Le Suisse (Ch.86-14), was arrested in 1664 when he attempted to abduct newly arrived immigrants to Canada to force them to work on his farm, probably as unpaid labour. He was convicted of kidnapping, fined 300 *livres* and banished from Quebec City for life. He was one of Theodore Seguin's 7th-great-grandfathers (on his father's side).

Recorded instances of sexual offences in the legal records of New France are uncommon, but they did occur [see Eric Wenzel, *La Justice Criminelle en Nouvelle-France 1670-1760*]. In 1668, one of Alphonsine's 7th-great-grandfathers (on her mother's side), Antoine GABOURY (Ch.186-14), was convicted of the attempted rape of 10-year-old Marie Jeanne Hébert. His punishment was to have his head shaved as a sign of shame, then publicly beaten and transported to France for nine years as a galley slave. Surprisingly, after completing his sentence, Gaboury returned to New France and started a family with the Seguin ancestor Jeanne MIGNAULT (Ch.186-15).

Another of Alphonsine's 7th-great-grandmothers (on her mother's side), Marie Renée LOPEZ (Ch.164-7), died in February, 1679, leaving her four unmarried daughters, ages 6 to 12, and her two young sons in the care of their father Jean VALIQUET *dit* Laverdure (Ch.164-6). In September of that year, Valiquet was arrested and convicted of incest. His initial sentence of death by hanging was commuted to banishment from Montreal for life. It is not known what happened to the younger children. They may have been taken in by the one married daughter, Marie Nicole VALIQUET (Ch.164-3) who had wed Louis LEDOUX earlier in 1679.

Yet another of Alphonsine's 7th-great-grandmothers, Marie-Vincente PACAUD (Ch.155-11) operated a bordello at Quebec City. That in itself was a crime, but she was also one of ten persons who, in 1675, was arrested for a robbery at Quebec City's Hôtel-Dieu hospital. Marie was convicted on both counts and sentenced to a public beating. Her husband, Simon CHAPACOU (Ch.159-5), also arrested in connection with these crimes, was not convicted. However, Marie-Vincente's accomplice in the robbery, Simon Raymond, was convicted and sentenced to death.

Unfortunately, murder among the *Canadiens* was not unknown. At Trois-Rivières, Que., in 1671, the 36-year-old ex-soldier, Julien Latouche, was murdered. At age 12, Elisabeth Isabelle BERTEAU (Ch.159-5), a 6th-great-grandmother of Alphonsine Seguin, had married Latouche the year before. While the marriage of girls at such a young age was not uncommon at the time, such a great age difference between husband and wife was somewhat unusual. Latouche turned out to be a brutal husband who often beat his child-bride. After enduring his beatings for a year, Elisabeth conspired with

Broken on the wheel prior to execution, 1694.   The condemned man is tied to a wheel and his limbs are broken by the executioner wielding an iron rod. The priest stands above the man praying for his soul before the execution by hanging. Depending on the severity of the crime, the dead body might also be drawn and quartered.
["The Execution of Alexandre Dellguerre", Bibliothèque Nationale de France, ark:/12148/btv1b84069995]

her parents to murder Latouche. In 1672, after they tried, unsuccessfully, to poison him, he was beaten to death. [See Tanguay *A Traverse,* and McNelly] Elisabeth, along with her father Jacques BERTEAU (Ch.159-10) and mother Marie Gillette BANNE (Ch.159-11) were arrested, tried and convicted of the murder. Because of her young age, Elisabeth's death sentence was commuted. Her parents, however, were hanged. Two years later, Elisabeth married Noel LAURENCE (Ch.159-4).

In 1690, Jean Haudecoeur of Boucherville, Que., the first husband of Marie Madeleine MATHON (Ch.88-3), was executed for murder. He had killed the Montreal merchant, Francois Poignet. For his crime, Haudecoeur was sentenced to be broken on the wheel, then hanged. Two years after his execution, his widow married the Seguin ancestor, René DAIGNEAU (Ch.88-2). René and Marie Madeleine were Theodore's 5th-great-grandparents (on his father's side).

Sadly, some Seguin ancestors were also victims of serious crimes. Jean VERDON (Ch.95-14), a 7th-great-grandfather of Theodore Seguin (on his father's side), was one of these victims. In 1678, Jean's wife, Marguerite RICHER (Ch.95-15) conspired with Charles Combaud (presumably her lover), to murder Jean in his home at La Prairie, Que. Combaud was arrested, tried and convicted of murder and sentenced to death. His accomplice, Marguerite, was tried and sentenced *in absentia* as she had fled the country, leaving her newborn son and her 1-year-old daughter, Marie Marguerite VERDON (the Seguin ancestor) as orphans. The young children were adopted by the childless couple, Mathurin Lelièvre and Marguerite Jasselin.

Toussaint HUNAULT *dit* Deschamps (Ch.108-8), a 7th-great-grandfather of Theodore Seguin (on his mother's side), was also a murder victim. In 1690, Gabriel Dumont de Balignac, an officer in the *Troupes de la Marine* stationed at Montreal, got into an altercation with Toussaint. The officer drew his sword and mortally stabbed Hunault. Dumont de Balignac then fled back to France to avoid prosecution for his crime. Records show that the murderer later served aboard a frigate in the French navy but he was never arrested for the crime he had committed in Canada. [Fournier, p.348]

Dispelling the Catholic Myth

While there is no doubt that the vast majority of the ancestors of Theodore Seguin and Alphonsine Seguin were Roman Catholics from France, the presence of individuals in their family tree who originated from other countries and who adhered to other religions indicates that the Seguin bloodline may not be as religiously pure as many Seguin descendents may have believed it to be. The family tree of Theodore and Alphonsine includes many Protestants from France, England, Belgium, Switzerland and Germany in addition to the Indigenous North Americans who practiced paganism, (some of whom were later converted to Christianity).

The English ancestors, all of whom immigrated to North America in the 17th Century, include Catherine LAWLOR (Ch.180-11), a *fille du Roi* from London, England; Suzanne BETFER (Bedford) (Ch.142-15) identified as a *fille à marier* from Gloucester, England, and Abel Joseph BARBE (Ch.84-2) from London, England, who joined the *Troupes de la Marine* in New France. In addition, there were members of the Allen, Kimball, Painter and Lamberton families (Ch.106), all of whom were Puritans who had fled England due to religious persecution and settled in the English colony of Massachusetts, and whose descendant, Sarah ALLEN (Ch.106-3), was later captured during the raid on Deerfield, Massachusetts, and taken to Montreal where she converted to Roman Catholicism.

Three immigrants from Switzerland, one from Belgium, and one from Germany are also part of the Seguin family tree. All of them would likely have been raised in Protestant families. André BADEL (Ch.173-14), a soldier in the Carignan-Salières Regiment, and his wife Barbe DUCHESNE (Ch.173-15), a *fille du Roi*, were both natives of Geneva, Switzerland. Pierre MIVILLE *dit* Le Suisse (Ch.86-14) had migrated from Fribourg, Switzerland to western France where he married Charlotte MAUGER, had 6 children, then emigrated to New France. Marie Anne BASMONT (Ch.170-5), born in Flanders in what was then the Spanish Netherlands (now Belgium), was a *fille du Roi* who arrived in Canada in 1673. Gebhardt NIEDING from the German state of Hesse-Hanau arrived as a soldier in 1777.

Alphonsine Seguin would probably have been surprised, and perhaps disappointed, to find that several Seguin ancestors who emigrated directly to Canada from France were not Roman Catholics. Instead, they were Protestants who had been raised in the Calvinist church. The Calvinists in France, also called Huguenots, had split from the Catholic Church in the early 16th Century. Religious tensions between Catholics and Protestants resulted in armed conflict — the French Wars of Religion — from 1562 until 1598. When King Henry IV of France pronounced the Edict of Nantes in 1598, giving Calvinists legal status and allowing them freedom of worship without official persecution, open warfare ended but French society remained divided along religious lines. However, hostilities between Catholics and Protestants broke out again in 1610 and continued until King Louis XIV removed the rights of Calvinists when he revoked the Edict of Nantes in 1685. It was in this environment of religious strife that many Calvinists left France, some with hopes for a better life in Canada.

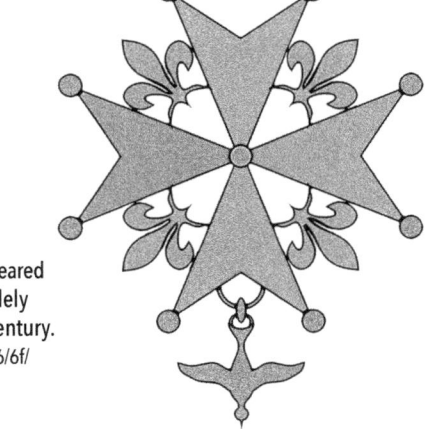

The Huguenot Cross.
This symbol of the French Calvinists first appeared in France in the late 17th Century and was widely adopted by French Protestants in the 19th Century.
[https://upload.wikimedia.org/wikipedia/commons/6/6f/Huguenot_cross.svg]

It has been estimated that more than 850 non-Catholics settled in New France over the course of the 17th and early 18th centuries. [Bédard, p.328] While there were early attempts by enterprising Protestant merchants — including Samuel de Champlain — to establish trading posts and settlements in New France, the immigration of Protestants to the colony was prohibited by *la Compagnie des Cents-Associés* in 1627. However, non-Catholics still settled in Canada and in Acadia. Many, including Champlain himself, converted to Catholicism before leaving France, but others never converted. Fearing persecution, many of these non-Catholics still participated in Roman Catholic rites in New France in order to keep their true religious beliefs concealed from their neighbours. Those who chose to neither hide their religious beliefs nor convert were usually tolerated in New France, but they did not enjoy all of the same rights as Catholic colonists.

Historical documents show that at least fifteen Seguin ancestors who emigrated from France had been baptized in or married in a Calvinist temple (see page 52). Undoubtedly, the religion of many more immigrants was not recorded or they hid their religious beliefs altogether.

TABLE 7 – French Calvinist Ancestors in New France

Name	Origin	Arrival in New France
Suzanne DENOYON (Ch.429-3)	Rouen, France	C.1649
Julien DOBIGEON (Ch.98-10)	Bretagne, France	1653
Perrine MONIER (Ch.98-11)	Bretagne, France	1653
Anne GODIN (Ch.81-7	La Rochelle, France	C.1654
Marie Esther RAMAGE (Ch.81-15)	La Rochelle, France	C.1654
Elie GODIN (Ch.81-14)	Saintonge, France	C.1654
Suzanne ROCHETEAU (Ch.80-5)	La Rochelle, France	C.1661
Marguerite DOUCINET (Ch.121-11)	La Rochelle, France	1662
Jean-Baptiste Denoyon (Ch.73-6)	Rouen, France	C.1662
Marie ARDION (Ch.517-7)	La Rochelle, France	1663
Anne JARNET (Ch.88-11)	France	C.1663
Isaac DODIN (Ch.88-10)	Ile de Ré, France	C.1663
Hélène DODIN (Ch.88-5)	La Rochelle, France	C.1663
Elie DUSSAULT (Ch.123-12)	La Rochelle, France	C.1663
Marie HUS (Ch.118-13)	Rouen, France	1667

Le Pays d'en Haut and *Le Détroit*

In the 17th Century, the *Canadiens* living along the St. Lawrence River referred to the Great Lakes region of North America as *le Pays d'en Haut,* the Upper Country; the vast region of forests and lakes upstream of Montreal that was then the domain of many Indigenous peoples and through which travelled, from time to time, small numbers of French missionaries, fur-traders and explorers.

One of Theodore Seguin's 8th-great-grandfathers (on his mother's side), Jean NICOLET (Ch.444-6) (see *Appendix A-3*), is said to have been one of the first Europeans to live in *le Pays d'en Haut*. Nicolet had arrived in New France in 1618. The following year, under instructions from Samuel de Champlain, the 21-year-old Nicolet travelled up the Ottawa River and stayed for two years with the Algonquins on Allumette Island before moving on to Lake Nipissing where he settled among the Anishinaabe Nipissing people (Nibissinineyug). He lived there until 1628 to learn their language and to establish a fur-trading partnership between the Nipissings and *la Compagnie des Cents-Associés*. After the death of his Nipissing wife, Gisis BAHMAHMAADJIMIWIN (see p.13), he returned to Quebec City with his infant daughter, Marie Madeleine Euphrosine NICOLET (Ch.123-13), and left her with the Ursuline nuns to be educated.

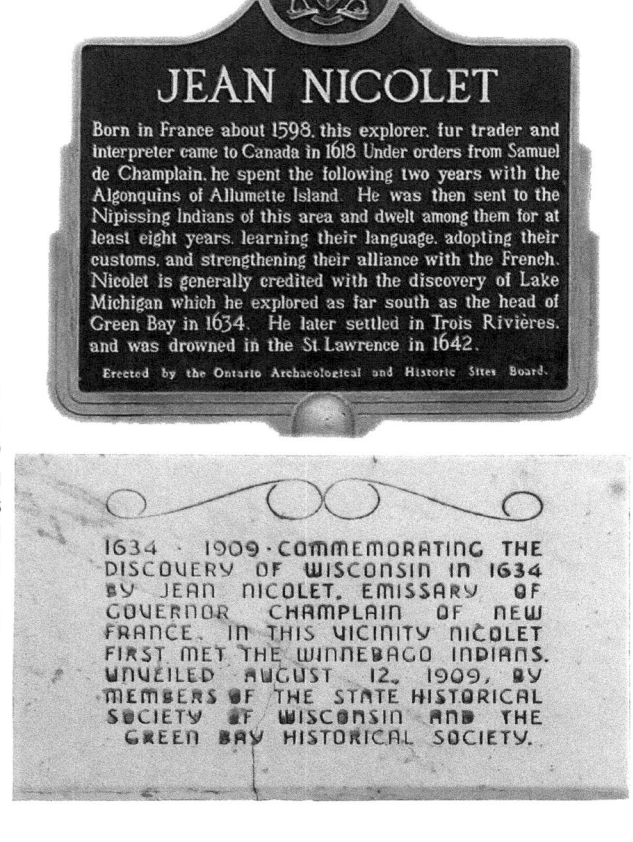

Plaques Commemorating the 17th Century Explorations of Jean Nicolet. These two plaques, erected in Ontario (1959) and Wisconsin (1909), are among more than 30 such plaques and markers found throughout the United States and Canada. The wording reflects the times in which they were created.
[The Historical Marker Database, www.hmdb.org]

New France and *Le Pays d'en Haut*, 1703.
The "Upper Country" was the vast territory that stretched west of Montreal to the Mississippi River and beyond.

- Lower left – the territory of the Pawnee (*Panis*), where Jean-Baptiste PRÉVERT and Nicolas DOYON were born.
- Bottom left – the village of Kaskaskia (*Caskoukia*) where several Seguin ancestors settled.
- West of Lake Michigan (*Lac des Illinois*) – the *Baie des Puans* (Green Bay) where Jean NICOLET encountered the Winnebego peoples.
- Centre right – the territory of the Nipissing peoples (*Nipissirniens*) where Nicolet's wife, Gisis BAHMAHMAADJIMIWIN, lived and where her daughter Marie Madeleine Euphrosine NICOLET was born.
- Right of centre – *Le Détroit*.
- North shore of Lake Ontario – the abandoned Iroquois villages are shown.
- Eastern end of Lake Ontario – Fort Frontenac (*Cataracoui*).
- South of Lake Ontario – Iroquois (Haudenosaunee) territory stretching east to the Hudson River valley.

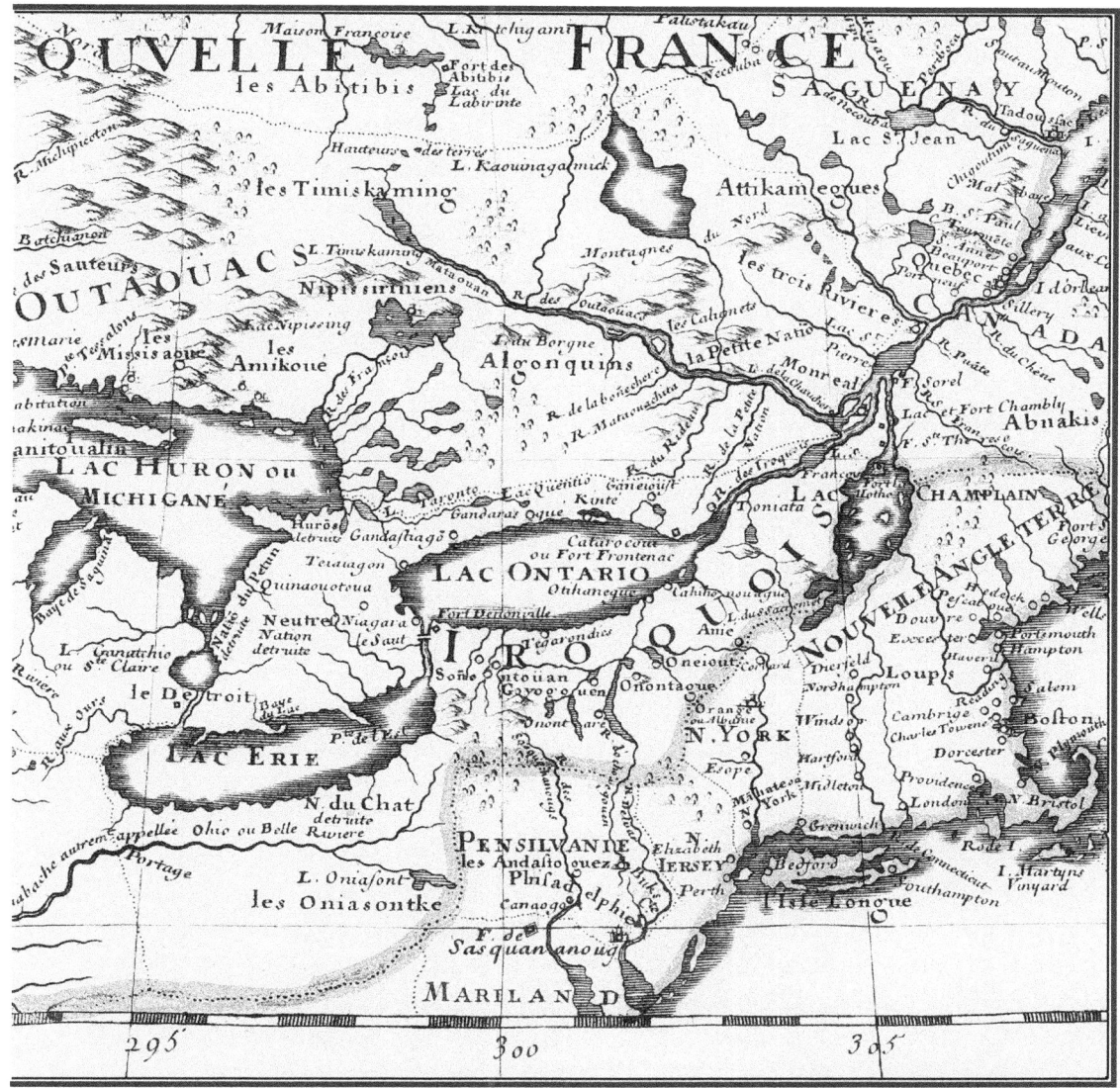

["Carte du Canada ou de la Nouvelle France" (detail) by Guillame Del'Isle. Published, Paris, 1708. Courtesy of the David Rumsey Map Collection, no.4764.097.]

Around 1634, Nicolet was sent further west. He guided Jesuit missionaries to Georgian Bay where they started construction of the Ste. Marie mission to the Wendat, situated near the present site of Midland, Ont. [http://www.biographi.ca/en/bio/nicollet_de_belleborne_jean_1E.html] In the first half of the 17th Century, the Wendat were an important fur-trading ally of the French, but their numbers were greatly reduced by disease (especially smallpox brought by Europeans) and, by 1650, they had been dispersed from their traditional lands after being nearly exterminated by the Iroquois; an action which, in the 21st Century, would be labelled as genocide.

Nicolet proceeded up Georgian Bay, along the north shore of Lake Huron and past the rapids at Sault Ste. Marie. On the shores of Lake Superior, he encountered people of the Siouan-speaking Winnebago (Hoocagra) nation who called him *Manitouiriniou.** He also may have explored as far south as Green Bay (Baie des Puans), Wisconsin. Before returning to Quebec City, Nicolet formed an alliance with the Winnebagos for the purpose of trading furs and for mutual protection against the Iroquois Confederacy.

Other explorers seeking a water route to the Pacific Ocean or in search of more fur-trading opportunities followed in Nicolet's footsteps. One of these explorers was Médard Chouart des Groseilliers whose expedition to *le Pays d'en Haut* included Claude DAVID (Ch.111-12), a 7th-great-grandfather of Theodore Seguin (on his mother's side). Claude had arrived in New France around 1646, and worked as a gunsmith at Trois-Rivières, Que. Groseilliers needed a man with Claude DAVID's skills on this expedition to Lake Superior, so Claude left his pregnant wife with their four young sons, ages 3 to 9 years, in Trois Rivières and journeyed to Montreal from where the expedition left for the Upper Country in the summer of 1659, returning the following year.**

More than three decades of unrelenting attacks on the settlements of New France by the Five Nations Confederacy were followed by a dozen years of uneasy peace between the French and the Iroquois. This peace was the result of the show of force by the Carignan-Salières Regiment and their incursions into Mohawk territory in 1666 combined with the weakening of the Haudenosaunee populations from European diseases. This break in hostilities spurred the proliferation of Christian missions and French fur-trading posts in *le Pays d'en Haut*. In 1668, Sulpician priests started a mission at Kentio, the Cayuga village in what is now Prince Edward County, Ont. Two years later, missionaries could be found at Iroquois villages on the Ganaraska River (Port Hope, Ont.) and on the Humber River (Toronto, Ont.). Much further west, in 1671, the Jesuits established missions at St. Ignace at the Straits of Mackinaw and on Green Bay on the west side of Lake Michigan. Fur-trading posts and Christian missions continued to spread westward, eventually as far as the Mississippi River, and then as far south as the Gulf of Mexico in a region that became known as *la Louisiane.* At least one Seguin ancestor, Pierre PERTHUIS (Ch.135-2), is known to have gone as far south at Pointe Coupée, Louisiana (north of present-day Baton Rouge). He was Alphonsine Seguin's 5th-great-grandfather (on her father's side).

In 1673, a fortified fur-trading post, Fort Frontenac, was built by the French at Cataraqui (now Kingston, Ont.), and a number of Seguin ancestors would be stationed there over the following decades. Michel MESSIER *dit* St. Michel (Ch.162-4)

---

* See Marcel Trudel, "Jean Nicollet dans le lac Supérior et non dans le lac Michigan", *Revue d'histoire de l'Amerique français*, 34-2, 1980, and Jacques Gagnon, "Jean Nicolet au lac Michigan: Histoire d'une erreur historique", *Revue d'histoire de l'Amerique français*, 50-1, 1996.]

** Some sources show that Claude DAVID left Trois-Rivières in 1660 and returned three years later, but the birth date of his last child does not fit with those findings! [http://www.biographi.ca/en/bio/david_claude_1E.html]

was an officer in the Montreal militia who was with Governor La Barre's expedition to Iroquois country when they gathered their forces at Fort Frontenac in 1684. Michel knew the Iroquois well as he had been captured by them on two separate occasions and had survived both experiences. (see *Appendix A-15*) At Cataraqui, he was placed in charge of the sailing barque, *Le Général*. [www.biographi.ca/en/bio/messier_michel_2F.html] Michel MESSIER was Alphonsine's 6th-great-grandfather (on her mother's side).

Two soldiers of the *Troupes de la Marine*, both 5th-great-grandfathers of Theodore Seguin, were also likely stationed at Fort Frontenac: Pierre BIROLEAU (Ch.78-2) C.1692, who served under Captain Daniel Greysolon Dulhut, and Joseph POIRIER (Ch.100-2) C.1705, serving under Captain Jean-Louis Lacorne de Chaptes. Around 1720, another soldier, Louis GILBERT *dit* Comtois, (Ch.181-2), under the command of Captain Francois de Sales Amariton, would be posted much further west, to the fort at Green Bay (*Baie des Puans*) in what is now Wisconsin.*

By 1680, forts had also been built at the mouth of the Niagara River and on the St. Joseph River in south-western Michigan. In 1701, as peace negotiations between the Haudenosaunee and thirty-five other Indigenous nations and tribal confederacies were taking place, and which would result in the "Great Peace of Montreal", an officer in the *Troupes de la Marine*, Antoine Laumet de Lamotte Sieur de Cadillac, was building Fort Pontchartrain du Détroit (also known as Fort Detroit) on the narrow strait that connects Lake Huron and Lake Erie, *le Détroit du Lac Erié*. This is where the city of Detroit, Michigan now stands. It was in this region that a large number of Seguin descendants would settle and raise families from the 18th Century right through to the present day. The first ancestors of Theodore and Alphonsine to settle at *le Détroit* likely accompanied Cadillac in 1701. Among these were Pierre MALLET (b.1676) (Ch.135-6) and René DAIGNEAU (Ch.88-2).

The historical record shows that, by 1706, Pierre MALLET was living at Fort Pontchartrain with his wife, Marie Madeleine TUNÉ *dit* Dufresne and three young children. [Burton, p.11] Pierre and Marie Madeleine were Alphonsine's 6th-great-grandparents (on her father's side) (see *Appendix A-16*). At Montreal in 1716, their daughter, Marie Catherine MALLET, married Pierre PERTHUIS (b.1691) (Ch.135-2) and they also settled at Detroit. The MALLET and PERTHUIS families were both involved in the fur-trade, and by the 1730's they had all moved further west to the thriving fur-trading post and mission in the "Illinois Country" at Kaskaskia, which had been established C.1700 on the east bank of the Mississippi River, south of present-day St. Louis, Missouri.

René DAIGNEAU first appears in Detroit church records in 1705, when he married his second wife, Anastasie, an Anishinaabe Illinois woman. More than 200 years later, the last of the Seguins to migrate from Quebec and settle in the Detroit River region

---

* The locations of these soldiers is based on their year of arrival in New France together with the known postings of their company captains. [See Marcel Fournier, *Les Officiers de Troupes de la Marine au Canada, 1683-1760*.]

TABLE 1 – ANCESTORS OF *LA GRANDE RECRUE*, 1653

PURE LAINE – THREADS OF SEGUIN FAMILY HISTORY

TABLE 8 – MIGRANTS TO THE DETROIT RIVER REGION AND THE UPPER COUNTRY

NAME	MIGRATED	NOTES	CHART
René DAIGNEAU (Theodore's 5th-great-grandfather)	C.1705	d. 1730, Detroit	88
Pierre MALLET (Alphonsine's 6th-great-grandfather)	C.1706	d. C.1739, Kaskaskia, IL	135
- wife, M.Madeleine TUNÉ *dit* Dufresne		d. C.1739, Detroit	
- daughter, M.Catherine MALLET		Migrated further west, C.1743, with her husband, Pierre PERTHUIS (below). d. C.1745, Kaskaskia, IL ?	
Pierre ROBERT *dit* Lafontaine (Alphonsine's 6th-great-grandfather)	1706	His wife, M.Angelique PTOLOMÉE and children joined him in 1708 d. C.1713, Detroit	137
Jacques CAMPEAU (Alphonsine's 5th-great-grandfather)	1708	d. 1751, Detroit	134
Marie Angelique PTOLOMÉE (Alphonsine's 6th-great-grandmother)	1708	She joined her husband, Pierre ROBERT, in Detroit in 1708. d. 1744, Detroit	137
- daughter, Angelique ROBERT		She returned to the Montreal area C.1720. Her daughter, M.Anne PEPIN (below), migrated to Detroit C.1740. d. 1783, Boucherville, Que.	
Cécile CATIN (wife of Jacques CAMPEAU) (Alphonsine's 5th-great-grandmother)	C.1712	Joined her husband, Jacques CAMPEAU, at Detroit C.1712. She returned to Montreal where and gave birth to her 7th child just before dying there in 1715	134
- son, J.B. CAMPEAU		d. 1783, Detroit	
Louis MALLET (Theodore's 4th-great-grandfather)	C.1715	Went to Detroit, probably to work with his brother, Pierre MALLET (above). Louis arrived in Detroit sometime after the birth of his last child in 1714. d. 1717, Detroit	10
Pierre PERTHUIS *dit* Lalime (Alphonsine's 5th-great-grandfather)	C.1718	After settling in Detroit with his family, he moved further west and was residing at Kaskaski, Illinois, C.1743. He died at Pointe Coupée, Lousianna, 1758.	135
Jean-Baptiste PRÉVERT ‡ (Theodore's 5th-great-grandfather)	C.1725	d. C.1727, somewhere in the Upper Country	95
- wife, M.Genevieve Anne DESFORGES *dit* St. Maurice		d. C.1744, Kaskaskia, IL	
Marie Anne (Louise) PEPIN *dit* Descardonnets (Alphonsine's 4th-great-grandmother)	C.1740	Migrated to the Detroit area, C.1740 and probably stayed with her uncle, Antoine ROBERT. m. 1744, at Detroit, Pierre BOYER d. 1795, Detroit	18
Pierre BOYER (Alphonsine's 4th-great-grandfather)	C.1740	m. 1744, at Detroit, Marie Anne PEPIN d. 1765, Detroit	18
Joseph SEGUIN *dit* Laderoute (Alphonsine's 3rd-great-grandfather)	**C.1750**	m. 1751, at Detroit, Marie Therese TREMBLAY d. 1795, Detroit	**18**
Pierre TREMBLAY (Alphonsine's 4th-great-grandfather)	C.1750	Settled at Fox Creek, Grosse Pointe, MI. d. 1763, Detroit	18
- wife, Madeleine SIMARD *dit* Lombrette		d. 1750, Detroit	
- daughter, Marie Therese TREMBLAY		m. 1751, at Detroit, Joseph SEGUIN d. 1800, Detroit	

TABLE 8 – MIGRANTS (CONTINUED)

Name	Migrated	Notes	Chart
Joseph Amable DELIÈRES *dit* Bonvouloir (Alphonsine's 4th-great-grandfather)	C.1760	Migrated with his wife, and his mother, Marie Marthe DARAGON. d. 1806, Sandwich, Ont	21
- wife, Veronique VERONNEAU *dit* Denis		d. 1773, Assumption, Sandwich, Ont.	
Marie Marthe DARAGON *dit* Lafrance (Alphonsine's 5th-great-grandmother)	C.1760	Probably migrated along with her son, Joseph Amable DELIÈRES. d. C.1777, Assomption du Detroit	156
Pierre LETOURNEAU (Alphonsine's 3rd-great-grandfather)	C.1780	Arrived in the Detroit River region sometime before he married Louise DELIÈRES in 1784. d. 1818, Sandwich, Ont.	21
Augustin MALBOEUF *dit* Beausoleil (Alphonsine's 4th-great-grandfather)	C.1795	Migrated to the Detroit River region sometime before the death of his 3rd child in 1795. d. 1812, Sandwich, Ont.	19
- wife, Monique BOUCHARD *dit* Lavallée		d. 1844, Sandwich, Ont.	
Joseph NOUVION *dit* Sanscartier (Alphonsine's 2nd-great-grandfather)	C.1805	Arrived in the Detroit River region sometime before his marriage to Angelique LETOURNEAU in 1808. d. 1828, Sandwich, Ont.	21
Léon CUSSON *dit* L'Ange (Alphonsine's great-grandfather)	C.1835	Arrived in the Detroit River region sometime before his marriage to Marie Louise NOUVION in 1837 d. 1853, Sandwich, Ont.	3
Méderic BRAULT *dit* Lafleur (Alphonsine's maternal grandfather)	C.1890	The 1891 Census of Canada shows him living in Essex County, Ontario, with his wife and 7 of his 11 children d. 1934, Tecumseh, Ont.	3
- wife, Marie Henriette BOUCHER *dit* Barbel		d. 1901, Tecumseh, Ont.	
- daughter, Delima BRAULT *dit* Lafleur		d. 1946, Windsor, Ont.	
George Napoleon SEGUIN (Theodore's father)	C.1925	d. 1940, Windsor, Ont.	2
- wife, Exilda POIRIER		d. 1942, Windsor, Ont.	
- son, Theodore Seguin		d. 1979, Windsor, Ont.	

would be René's 5th-great-grandson, Theodore Seguin (see *Appendix A-17*), who arrived at Windsor, Ont., with his parents and siblings sometime in the 1920's, and married Alphonsine Seguin, at Belle River, Ont. in 1926.

From the early 1700's to the mid-1920's, at least thirty-four of Theodore's and Alphonsine's direct ancestors migrated to the Detroit River region and the Upper Country from other parts of Canada; many arriving in the region several decades before the first ancestor bearing the Seguin name, Joseph SEGUIN *dit* Laderoute (b.1717) (Ch.18-4) arrived in the region. The table above lists those individuals.

Most of the migrants came from the heartland of New France — what is now the Province of Quebec — and they lived in the Detroit area, or across the river at Sandwich and Windsor, or on farms nearby in Essex County, Ont. Some migrated further west and spent their last days at distant fur-trade posts like those at Kaskaskia, Illinois and Pointe Coupée, Louisiana. Others settled in the Detroit area for only a short time before returning to Quebec.

Alphonsine's 3rd-great-grandfather, Joseph SEGUIN *dit* Laderoute (b.1717) (Ch.18-4), was the first direct ancestor bearing the Seguin name to settle at *le Détroit*. He was the fourth of six sons of Jean-Baptiste SEGUIN and Genevieve BARBEAU (Ch.18). Joseph was likely part of a group of twelve voyageurs who set out from Montreal in two canoes in the spring of 1748.* After the men received a licence from the governor of New France, Roland-Michel Barrin de la Galissionnière, permitting them to venture into *le Pays d'en Haut*, Joseph would have left his home on the south shore of the St. Lawrence River and paddled with his companions more than 1,000 kilometers westward to the village which had grown around Fort Pontchartrain du Détroit.

For nearly a century, the usual transportation route used by the French to voyage from Montreal to the Upper Country was by way of the Ottawa River, across the Mattawa River and Lake Nipissing, then down the French River to Georgian Bay. This would allow voyageurs to avoid the Iroquois who, by the mid-17th Century, not only occupied their traditional territory south of Lake Ontario, but they had forced other Indigenous peoples out of much of the area north of Lake Ontario and Lake Erie and claimed it as their own hunting and trapping grounds. However, the "Great Peace of Montreal" signed in 1701 by the French and thirty-nine Indigenous nations and tribal confederacies, including the Haudenosaunee, ended more than a century of warfare among the tribes. More importantly for the French, the Five Nations Confederacy had also agreed to remain neutral in any armed conflicts in North America between France and England. With the removal of the Iroquois threat, the more direct route from Montreal to Detroit — up the St. Lawrence River and along the north shore of lakes Ontario and Erie — became available. In fact, the voyageurs' licence to the Upper Country stipulated that they must travel that route and only follow the north shore of Lake Ontario to avoid the British in their fort on the south shore at Oswego. Furthermore, their licence prohibited them from engaging in any trading activities until they reached Detroit.

So, after portaging around the Lachine rapids at the western end of Montreal Island, Joseph SEGUIN and his companions would have paddled up the St. Lawrence River; portaging their canoes around five more sets of rapids that impeded their progress. After five days, they may have stopped at the mission of La Présentation (now Ogdensburg, NY) where a new fort was under construction. From there, they continued upriver, likely stopping at Fort Frontenac (Kingston, Ont.) before proceeding through the Bay of Quinte. After portaging their canoes across the Carrying Place

---

* See BANQ, *Rapport de l'Archiviste de la province de Québec, 1922-1923*, p.230. In the original document dated 18 March, 1748, Joseph's surname is obscured. Further research may be required to confirm that this was Joseph Seguin *dit* Laderoute. It is also possible that Joseph arrived in 1750 with a group of 20 men in 4 canoes [see licence issued 10 June, 1750, BANQ *Enregistrement d'une permission accordée par Jacques-Pierre Taffanel de la Jonquière, gouverneur de la Nouvelle-France, le 8 juin, à Moisan, de quatre canots et vingt hommes, pour se rendre au Poste de Détroit*].

to Wellers Bay (Prince Edward County, Ont.), another four or five days of paddling along the north shore of Lake Ontario would take them past the abandoned Iroquois villages at Ganaraske (Port Hope, Ont.), Gandatsetiagon (Pickering, Ont.), and Teia-iagon (Toronto, Ont.). Then, to avoid the daunting portage around Niagara Falls, they would have entered Burlington Bay at the western end of the lake and followed a well-known overland route of more than twenty kilometers, dragging their canoes through shallow creeks and portaging over the height of land to the Grand River, which took them down to Lake Erie. Along the north shore of that lake, short portages across Long Point and Point Pelee were made before reaching the mouth of the Detroit River. Some six or seven weeks after leaving home,* Joseph SEGUIN would have arrived at *le Détroit du Lac Erié*, a settlement of only ninety-six families, totalling fewer than five hundred inhabitants. [LAC, series G1, v.461, p.28] There, he likely worked as a fur-trade outfitter in the employ of his aging uncle and namesake, Joseph Seguin *dit* Laderoute (b.1694), who had settled at Detroit twenty-five years earlier and where he had married Francoise Sauvage in 1723. By 1751, the younger Joseph himself would be married to 17-year-old Marie-Thérèse TREMBLAY (Ch.18-5)who had arrived at Detroit with her parents around the same time as her new husband.

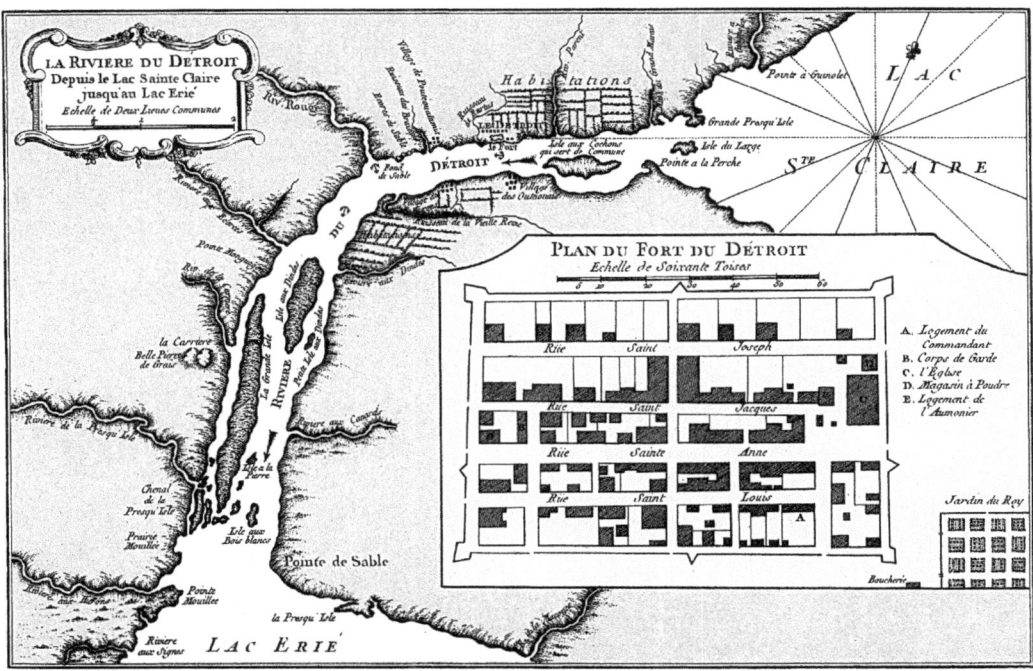

The Detroit River Region in 1752. Map, "*La Riviere du Détroit...*" drawn in 1752, and *Plan du Fort du Détroit* drawn in 1749, by Gaspard Chaussegros de Léry. [University of Michigan Library Digital Collections, no.013395736]

---

* Transit time from Montreal to Detroit is based on estimates provided by expert Canadian canoeist David R. Rowney, in conjunction with various historical accounts.

While it is rare to find the Seguin name in the early historical records for Detroit, many documents contain the name "Laderoute", and several surveys made of the region over the next sixty years show a number of ribbon farms east of Fort Detroit marked with the name "Laderoute" as well as names of many other Seguin ancestors. Gaspard Chaussegros de Léry, a French military engineer, drew several maps of the Detroit River region in 1752. One detailed map shows two adjoining lots several kilometers east of Fort Detroit labelled "Laderoute *père*" (four arpents by forty arpents) and "Laderoute *fils*" (2 arpents by forty arpents). [Dunnigan, p.45] "Laderoute *père*" was certainly the elder Joseph Seguin *dit* Laderoute (b.1694) who lived there with his wife, Francoise Sauvage, and their children. He had been granted the 135-acre lot opposite the eastern end of Ile aux Cochons (now Belle Isle) in 1734, by the governor of New France. ["Acte de concession", July 13, 1734. BANQ: E1,S3,P280] The adjacent lot was probably owned by his oldest son, Cajétan, a 1st-cousin of Alphonsine's direct ancestor, Joseph SEGUIN *dit* Laderoute (b.1717). While the back half of these ribbon farms (north of what is now Jefferson Avenue in Detroit), once cleared, would have been productive agricultural lands, the front half running down to the Detroit River was marshy, part of the extensive *Grand Marais* (the Great Marsh) that stretched along the river from Ile aux Cochons to Grosse Pointe on Lake St. Clair.

In 1796, when British surveyor Patrick McNiff drew his map of the Detroit River region (opposite), he marked three lots belonging to members of the Seguin *dit* Laderoute family: Joseph Laderoute (Lot 39), "Widow" Laderoute (Lot 41) and Pierre Laderoute (Lot 53). Since the elder Joseph (b.1694) had died more than 40 years earlier, and his son, whose name was also Joseph (b.1730), had died in 1751, lots 39 and 41 could only have been the property of Alphonsine's direct ancestors. However, Joseph SEGUIN *dit* Laderoute (b.1717), had died in 1795, the year before the McNiff

View of Detroit from the river in 1796.   Detail of inset from "Plan Topographique du Détroit...", drawn by Philippe-Joseph Létombe, 1796. [Service Historique de l'Armée de Terre, France. no.7-B-61]   [see Dunnigan, p.60]

survey, so Lot 39 would have passed to his son, Joseph SEGUIN *dit* Laderoute (b.1764) and his wife Archange CAMPEAU, Alphonsine's 2nd-great-grandparents. Lot 41 would have been the property of the widow, Marie-Therese TREMBLAY, Alphonsine's 3rd-great-grandmother. Marie-Therese's younger son, Pierre, was the owner of Lot 53, two kilometers further east along the river.

By 1810, we find Marie-Therese's older son, Joseph SEGUIN *dit* Laderoute (b.1764) still living on the same lot, although the Michigan Territory surveyor, Aaron Greely, had renumbered it as Lot 724. Greely's map also shows the adjacent land, Lot 723, as belonging to Joseph's brother, Jean-Baptiste Seguin *dit* Laderoute. [Dunnigan, p.45]

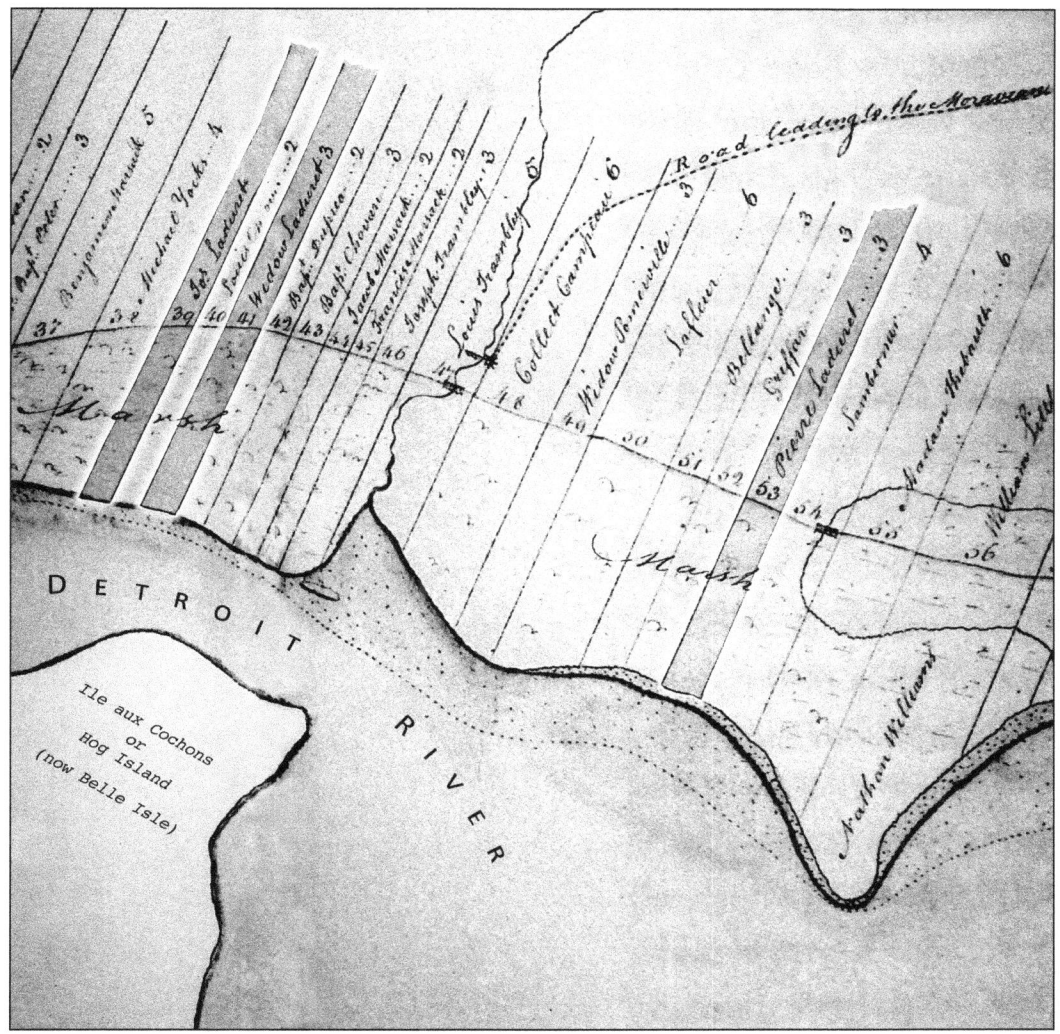

"A Plan of the settlements at Detroit and its vicinity..." (detail).
Surveyed and drawn by Patrick McNiff, Detroit, 1796.
[From Dunnigan, pp. 106-107. In the collection of the Clements Library, University of Michigan, Ann Arbor. Map Division, 6-N-12]

Over the course of the six decades during which these surveys were made, the people of the Detroit River region saw many changes in boundaries and allegiances. In 1760, after the Governor of New France had capitulated to the British Army, British soldiers of the 60th Royal American Regiment and Rogers Rangers occupied Fort Detroit. By the Treaty of Paris three years later, France ceded its colony of Louisiana to Spain, and its colony of Canada to Great Britain. This new British territory included all of the settlements in the St. Lawrence valley as well as much of present-day southern Ontario and the state of Michigan. The *Canadien* residents of Detroit were then British subjects in a colony that, from 1774 to 1791, was called Quebec.

By 1783, as a result of the American War of Independence, Great Britain had lost thirteen of its North American colonies to the newly formed United States of America. Officially, Detroit then became part of the United States, but it remained under British control, administered as part of the Province of Upper Canada until 1796. When Detroit was finally handed over to the Americans, many Seguin ancestors in the Detroit River region would have been required to swear allegiance to the United States. By 1805, the U.S. Government had divided up its old Northwest Territory to create new political divisions including Michigan Territory, with Detroit as its capitol.

Several of Theodore's and Alphonsine's ancestors in the Detroit River region would have witnessed first-hand all of these political changes of the late 18th and early 19th centuries. People like Joseph Amable DELIÈRES (Ch.21-14), his son-in-law Pierre LETOURNEAU (Ch.21-6), Jean-Baptiste CAMPEAU (Ch.18-6) and his wife Marie Catherine BOYER (Ch.18-7), and Joseph SEGUIN's wife, Marie-Therese TREMBLAY (Ch.18-5) would have lived through these tumultuous times.

When the War of 1812 broke out, allegiances would be tested. Some Seguin ancestors living on the American side of the Detroit River likely sided with the British who occupied Detroit from August 1812, until September, 1813, while others sided with the United States or remained neutral. (see *Appendix C*)

By 1837, the year Michigan was admitted to the Union as the 26th state, the names Seguin and Laderoute had virtually disappeared from the maps and records of Detroit. Most of the male offspring of the elder Joseph Seguin (b.1694) had migrated further west to Indiana and Illinois, and some had moved across the river into Canadian territory. The male offspring of Alphonsine's direct ancestor, Joseph SEGUIN *dit* Laderoute (b.1717) had also moved to Canada. Only the family names of some of the other direct ancestors — the Boyers, Campeaus and Tremblays, to name a few— are still known on the American side of the border.

INTO THE 20TH CENTURY AND BEYOND

Despite the fact that Canada became part of the British Empire in 1763, at the end of the Seven Years War when France gave up its North American possessions (except for the islands of St. Pierre and Miquelon), life under British rule changed very little for the *Canadiens*. They continued to speak French; the French Civil Code remained as the basis of their legal system and, most importantly, they were allowed to continue to practice their Roman Catholic religion without official persecution. Daily life on the farms and in the villages of the St. Lawrence valley and the Detroit River region remained much as it had been during the French Regime.

Further political changes over the course of the 19th Century likewise had little effect on their lives. At the end of the American War of Independence in 1783, the settlement of American refugees (the Loyalists) in areas of British North America west of Montreal resulted, in 1791, in the division of the colony of Quebec into Upper Canada and Lower Canada. Fifty years later, these two colonies, renamed the provinces of Canada West and Canada East, were reorganized into the United Province of Canada. In 1867, the British government legislated the union of this province with Nova Scotia and New Brunswick to form the quasi-independent Dominion of Canada.

Sometime before 1822, Joseph SEGUIN *dit* Laderoute and his wife Archange CAMPEAU (Alphonsine's 2nd-great-grandparents) had moved across the Detroit River to Sandwich, the sprawling township in Essex County, Ont., largely made up of ribbon farms lining the south bank of the Detroit River. By the middle of the century, the

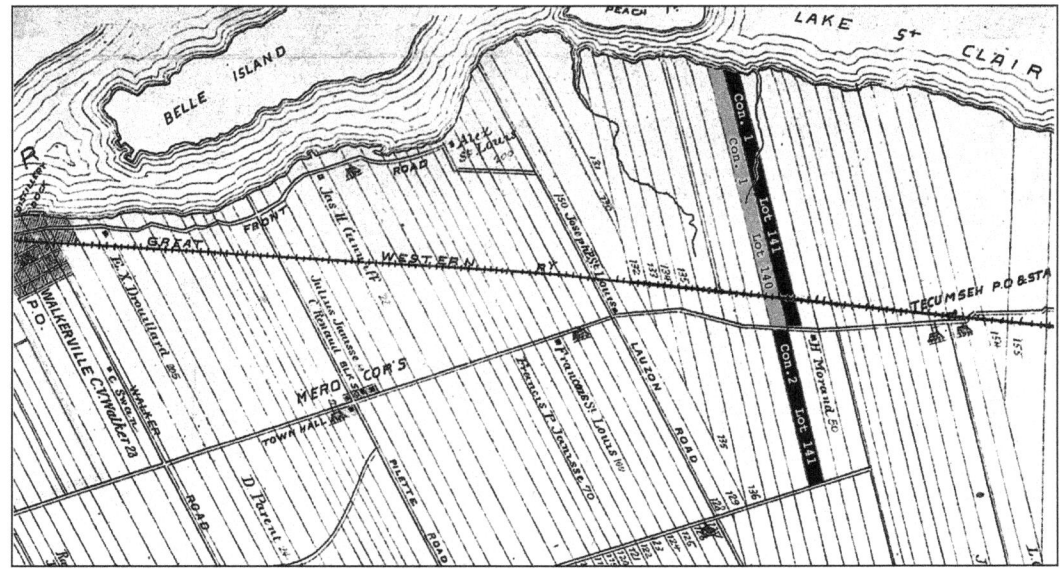

Three of the Seguin farms in Sandwich East Township (shown in black and grey), 1881,
Detail from Belden's *Historical Atlas of Essex & Kent Counties Ontario*. [H. Belden & Co., Toronto, 1881. E&W Sandwich, p.24]

township would be divided into East and West sections, and the towns of Windsor and Sandwich would be created. In Sandwich Township, Joseph and Archange joined a number of their children who had already settled and married there. Eventually, at least nine of their thirteen children would move to Canada. Their second son, Jean-Baptiste SEGUIN *dit* Laderoute, and his wife, Julie BEAUSOLEIL, Alphonsines's great-grandparents, owned a farm in Sandwich Township. This land, (Lot 141, Con.1, Sandwich East) fronting on the Tecumseh Road and running back to the Detroit River, was eventually acquired by their oldest son, Joseph SEGUIN *dit* Laderoute (b.1829) (Ch.3-4). This lot is shown on the previous page in *Belden's Atlas* of 1881.

Census data collected every ten years has given us intriguing snapshots of tiny portions of the lives of the Seguin family in Essex County. The 1851 Census of Canada West shows Jean-Baptiste and his wife Julie living in a 1-storey log house on Lot 141. At that time, their 130-acre property was mostly forested with some marshy areas — only fifteen acres were under cultivation with another five acres used as pasture for their four bulls, three milk cows, two calves, four horses and twelve sheep. A good portion of the family's income likely came from raising calves and selling them to other farmers. In addition, they had produced 500 barrels of pork in 1851, and there were still eight pigs in the piggery. That year, the farm also yielded forty bushels of wheat, ten bushels of barley, fifty bushels of oats, ten bushels of corn, ten bushels of potatoes, four tons of hay and fifteen pounds of tobacco, and the family produced twenty pounds of wool along with twenty-five yards of fulled cloth and fifteen pairs of socks. [1851 Census of the Province of Canada] The fruits of their labour would sustain the family of eleven children and provide a surplus which could be sold at the market in the nearby town of Tecumseh or traded for other goods and services.

Ten years later, the census shows that their eldest child, Joseph SEGUIN (b.1829), newly married to Marcelline CUSSON from nearby Pike Creek, Ont., had acquired a 40-acre property on the other side of the Tecumseh Road, Lot 140, Concession 2, where he had built his own 1-storey log house.

By 1871, Joseph's parents, Jean-Baptiste and Julie, were living with four of their adult children on the 75-acre property (Lot 140, Con. 1) next to their original farm. It seems that Joseph was now in possession of his father's farm on Lot 141 which, by that time, had been improved considerably. The census for that year shows that there were now two separate

Marcelline Cusson, 1931.
[Obituary, "Pioneer Passes",
The Windsor Star, 23 March 1931, p.5]

houses on the property. Joseph and Marcelline lived in one of the houses with their six children (including Philippe SEGUIN, Alphonsine's father). Another five children would eventually be raised there. The property also included a barn, a stable for their six horses, and a shed in which they kept a carriage, a sleigh, two wagons, a fanning mill and two ploughs.

The farm was no longer in the cow/calf business, but had expanded considerably into cash crops. The acreage under cultivation had been quadrupled over the course of twenty years, and those sixty acres now yielded 600 bushels of corn, 500 bushels of oats, 100 bushels of wheat, eighty bushels of barley, sixty bushels of potatoes, fifty bushels of peas and thirty bushels of apples. In addition, Joseph had harvested seventy-five bushels of rye which he may have sold to Hiram Walker who had opened his whiskey distillery twelve years earlier, just a half-day's wagon ride away on the Canadian side of the Detroit River in what would become the town of Walkerville.

In 1871, the farm also produced two bushels of grass seed, forty pounds of butter, forty pounds of wool and 300 cords of firewood. There were now twenty acres of pasture for the horses, two milk cows and twenty-four sheep. Twenty-seven pigs made up the rest of the livestock. Joseph and Marcelline, Alphonsine's paternal grand-parents, would raise their eleven children on that farm. Without a doubt, that Seguin family had become successful and prosperous farmers.

Just four farm lots further east along the Tecumseh Road, Alphonsine's maternal grandparents settled in 1885. Médéric BREAULT *dit* Lafleur and Henriette BOUCHER *dit* Lacroix were from Quebec's Lanaudière region north of Montreal. Sometime after the birth of their sixth child in 1877, the family had moved to Lowell, Massachusetts, where they joined other members of their extended family working in the Lowell textile mills. When they moved back to Canada several years later, they settled on a farm in Essex County, Ont.

Médéric Breault on his 90th Birthday, 1931.
Detail of photograph, "Mederic Breault Celebrates 90th Birthday With Surprise Party".
[*The Windsor Star*, 20 April 1931, p.16]

The principal hub of the farming community for French-Canadians in Essex County was the town of Tecumseh. Ste. Anne's Roman Catholic church was established there around 1860. In 1872, a large masonry church replaced the original wooden church building which was moved to one of the Seguin farms to be used as a barn. [https://catholicfamily.ca/history-of-ste-annes]

It was in the new church that Méderic and Henriette's daughter, Delima BREAULT *dit* Lafleur married Philippe SEGUIN *dit* Laderoute in 1891.

The Census of Canada later that year shows Philippe and Delima, Alphonsine's parents, living on Lot 141 in a 2-storey, 6-room house, which was a third dwelling that had been built on Joseph SEGUIN's property. Philippe's parents continued to live in the main house while his older brother, Jean-Baptiste, lived in the other house. Since Jean-Baptiste was destined to inherit the family farm on the death of their father, Philippe soon purchased his own farm — 100 acres in the 5th Concession of nearby Maidstone Township. Lot 16 included a small, wood frame house with a barn and a number of outbuildings.

Philippe Seguin and Delima Breault, c.1900
[W.A. Murdoch, photographer, Windsor, Ont. Author's collection]

The Farm of Philippe Seguin and Delima Breault, c.1930.
The farm was situated on Lot 16, Con. 5, Maidstone Township,
Essex County, Ont. [Hand-tinted photograph. Author's collection.]

This is where he and Delima raised their seven children, and this is where several of their grandchildren, including Alphonsine's sons Leonard and Philip (along with their cousin Donald Seguin), would later spend several weeks of their childhood summer vacations every year.

Back in the mid-18th Century, Alphonsine's ancestor Joseph SEGUIN (b.1717) had extended one branch of the Seguin family from Boucherville, Que., to the Detroit River region. At the same time, it was Joseph's older brother, Pierre, Theodore's ancestor, who was the progenitor of a separate branch of the family which, over the course of several generations, migrated up the Ottawa River valley, starting from Boucherville, then to Ste. Anne de Bellevue at the west end of Montreal Island, across the Lac de Deux Montagnes to Vaudreuil, Que., and up the Ottawa River to Oka, Rigaud, Papineauville, Perkins and finally to Thurso, Que., where Theodore, the second son of Napoleon SEGUIN* and Exilda POIRIER was born in 1904.

Napoleon Seguin and Exilda Poirier, C.1920
[E. Paul, photographer, Rockland, Ont. Author's collection]

By the 1920's, Canada had seen many changes. Five more provinces had been included in Confederation and the country had suffered through the Great War (1914-1918). Theodore had been too young to fight in the war, but several brothers, cousins and uncles of both Theodore and Alphonsine had been conscripted or volunteered and sent overseas. Now, with the country enjoying a time of peace and relative prosperity, Napoleon and Exilda decided to migrate from their Ottawa valley home to Windsor, Ont., with seven of their children, including Theodore.

In the backcountry outside of Thurso, Que., as a young man Theodore had worked in a lumber camp. In the largely agricultural region of their new home in Essex County, Ont., there were no lumber camps so, after arriving in Windsor, Theodore found work across the river as a bottle-washer with the Detroit pharmaceutical manufacturer, Parke Davis & Co. Even though his future wife, Alphonsine also worked at Parke Davis, the couple first met at a church function in the Windsor area. Unbeknownst to both of them, they were distant cousins. (see *Appendix A-1 & A-2*) In 1926, Alphonsine and Theodore were married at Belle River, Ont., in the Roman Catholic church of St. Simon and St. Jude.

---

* Napoleon was a son of distant cousins Eustache SEGUIN and Philomene DUQUETTE (see *Appendix A-19*).

Alphonsine Seguin and Theodore Seguin On Their Wedding Day,
June 22, 1926.
Standing: Alfred Seguin (brother of the groom), and Maria Seguin (sister of the bride).
[Photographer unknown. From the collection of Michelle Mailloux now in the author's possession.]

By 1931, they had two sons of their own and they had purchased a house on St. Pierre Street in Tecumseh, Ont. The house, valued at $3,000, was undoubtedly heavily mortgaged, for these were difficult times, socially and economically, for everyone. The census for that year indicates that the family could not even afford to have a radio in the house. As a married woman, Alphonsine was no longer allowed to work at Parke Davis, but as a hard-working mother and housewife she managed to raise six children through the Great Depression and the Second World War. Although the 1930's and 1940's were hard times, "...we had steak on the table every night for supper."*

After the arrival of their second child, Philip, they had moved into the city of Windsor. From the family home on Gladstone Avenue, Theodore could walk to the ferry at Walkerville where he would cross the Detroit River to the Parke Davis factory. When the family moved to 3811 Montcalm Ave. in Windsor's west end in 1942, he

---

* Recollections of Philip E. Seguin, as told, many times, to his children, Randall (Randy), Marc, Daniel (Dan), and Laurel.

would car-pool with a fellow worker who would drive to Detroit through the Detroit-Windsor tunnel. Theodore remained in the employ of Parke Davis right through to his retirement in 1969.

One minor but notable event in the family's life occurred in the 1950's when theirs became the first house on the block to have a television. Theodore had won the TV in a raffle and it became the focal point of the neighbourhood for quite some time. Often, dozens of neighbours and relatives of all ages could be seen huddled around the tiny black & white screen marvelling over the fuzzy images on the picture tube. The televised boxing matches were especially popular.

Alphonsine was an avid 5-pin bowler, and both she and Theodore loved playing cards at home, teaching their children and grandchildren games like euchre and cribbage. Even though they usually spoke French in the home, whenever they had anglophone guests visiting, French was forbidden, and only English was to be spoken until the guests departed. Unfortunately, their childrens' facility with French was not passed on to the next generation.

Each of their six surviving children* raised families of their own. Leonard married Shirley Macdonell and they raised eight children: Robert, Kenneth, Catherine,

Theodore and Alphonsine with five of their six children on their
35th Wedding Anniversary, 1961.
Left to right: Leonard, Alphonsine, Theodore, Jerome, Antoinette, Roger, Philip.
(Missing: Aline)
[Photographer unknown. Author's collection]

---

* Arthur, a son of Theodore and Alphonsine, b.1935, died in infancy.

Michael, Renée, Jeanne, Francis and Suzanne. The second son, Philip, married Loretta Ouellette (see *Appendix A-18*) whose first child, Matthew, was born prematurely and died within days of his birth. Four more children followed in quick succession: Randall Arthur, Marc Philip, Daniel Edward, and Laurel Teresa. Theodore and Alphonsine's third child, Antoinette, married Patrick Mailloux; their offspring included Michelle and three adopted children, Camille, Paul and Peter. Jerome, the third son, married Nancy Long and they raised three children: David, Andrea and Stephen. Theodore and Alphonsine's second daughter was Aline. After moving to California, she married Sidney Wanne and they adopted two boys: Allen and Thomas. The youngest of Theodore's and Alphonsine's children was Roger. He married Karen ___ , but after their son Jeffrey was born, the marriage was annulled. Later, Roger married Margaret Humphrey and together they raised her two children along with his own son.

Theodore and Alphonsine's **CHILDREN***, Grandchildren and Spouses – Family Reunion, 2002

1-Laurel [PHILIP], 2-Andrea [JEROME], 3-***ANTOINETTE**, 4-***PHILIP**, 5-***ROGER**, 6-Marc [PHILIP], 7-***JEROME**, 8-***LEONARD**, 9-David [JEROME], 10-Loretta Ouellette (Alphonsine's 3rd-cousin & wife of PHILIP), 11-Robert [LEONARD], 12-Paul [ANTOINETTE], 13-Francis [LEONARD], 14-Jeanne [LEONARD], 15-Catherine [LEONARD], 16-Randall [PHILIP], 17-Suzanne [LEONARD], 18-Michelle [ANTOINETTE], 19-***ALINE**, 20-Daniel [PHILIP], 21-Michael [LEONARD].

(MISSING: Kenneth [LEONARD], Renée [LEONARD], Camille Mailloux [ANTOINETTE], Peter Mailloux [ANTOINETTE], Stephen [JEROME], Allan Wanne [ALINE], Thomas Wanne [ALINE], Jeffery [ROGER].)

[Photographer unknown. Author's collection]

ℐ ℐ ℐ ℐ

Now, only tattered remnants of "*pure laine*" survive in the grandchildren and great-grandchildren of Theodore and Alphonsine Seguin. It is to the next generation that the torch has been passed to delve further into the roots of the Seguin family tree. In-depth archival research may serve to uncover more details that will allow us to gain a better picture of the lives of all of our ancestors, and add to the multitude of colourful threads that make up the myth of "*pure laine*".

Some of Theodore and Alphonsine's Great-Grandchildren– Family Reunion, 2002
[Photographer unknown. Author's collection]

ℐ ℐ ℐ ℐ

APPENDICES

Appendix A
Summary Lineages
77

Appendix B
Francois Seguin's Arrival in Canada
98

Appendix C
A War of 1812 Research Project
100

Appendix D
Dit Names
102

Appendix A

Summary Lineages

The complete Lineage Charts can be found in the volume
Pure Laine: The Lineage of Two Seguin Families (2004)
or downloaded at www.ontariohistory.ca/seguin.pdf .

A-1   5th-Cousins — Theodore Seguin & Alphonsine Seguin

A-2   6th-Cousins-once-removed – Theodore Seguin & Alphonsine Seguin

Indigenous Ancestry
A-3   – From Gisis Bahmahmaadjimiwin to Theodore Seguin
A-4   – From Marie Ouchistauichkoue Olivier to Alphonsine Seguin
A-5   – From Marie Madeleine St. Jean to Alphonsine Seguin
A-6   – From Jean-Baptiste Prévert to Theodore Seguin
A-7   – From Nicolas Doyon to Alphonsine Seguin

The First European Child
A-8   – From Hélène Desportes & Guillaume Hébert to Alphonsine Seguin
A-9   – From Hélène Desportes & Noel Morin to Alphonsine Seguin

A-10   The Plains of Abraham – From Abraham Martin to Alphonsine Seguin

A-11   A Founder of Montreal – From Léonard Lucos to Theodore Seguin

A-12   A German Soldier in America – From Gebhardt Nieding to Theodore Seguin

A-13   A Captive and 11th Cousins? – Marc Seguin & Marjorie Cluett

A-14   A Deerfield Captive – From Sarah Allen to Theodore Seguin

A-15   Twice Captured by the Iroquois – From Michel Messier to Alphonsine Seguin

Settlers at Detroit
A-16   – From Pierre Mallet to Alphonsine Seguin
A-17   – From René Daigneau to Theodore Seguin

A-18   3rd-Cousin to Her Mother-in-Law – Loretta Ouellette and Alphonsine Seguin

A-19   3rd-Cousins-once-removed – Eustache Seguin & Philomene Duquette

APPENDIX A — SUMMARY LINEAGES

APPENDIX A-1

5th-Cousins

Theodore Seguin & Alphonsine Seguin

Gen.						
IX	François **Seguin*** *m. 1672* Jeanne Petit	Ch.72		Ch.73	Jean-Baptiste **Barbeau*** *m. 1686* Marie Denoyon	
VIII		Jean-Baptiste **Seguin***	*m. 1710*	Geneviève **Barbeau***		Ch.10/18
VII	Pierre **Seguin*** *m. 1739* Marie Josephte Mallet	Ch.10	<--- siblings --->	Ch.18	Joseph **Seguin*** *m. 1751* Marie Therese Tremblay	
VI	Jean-Louis **Seguin*** *m. 1779* Josephte Brazeau	Ch.10	<--- 1st cousins --->	Ch.18	Joseph **Seguin*** *m. 1790* Archange Campeau	
V	Jean-Baptiste **Seguin*** *m. 1818* M.Louise Girard	Ch.2	<--- 2nd cousins --->	Ch.3	Jean-Baptiste **Seguin*** *m. 1829* Julie Beausoleil	
IV	Eustache **Seguin** *m. 1856* Philomene Duquette	Ch.2	<--- 3rd cousins --->	Ch.3	Joseph **Seguin*** *m. 1860* Marcelline Cusson	
III	Napoleon **Seguin** *m. 1895* Exilda Poirier	Ch.2	<--- 4th cousins --->	Ch.3	Philippe **Seguin*** *m. 1891* Delima Breault	
II		Theodore **Seguin**	<--- 5th cousins ---> *m. 1926*	Alphonsine **Seguin***		Ch.1
I	Leonard	Philip	Antoinette Jerome	Aline	Roger	Ch.1

*Barbeau *dit* Boisdoré   *Seguin *dit* Laderoute

APPENDIX A-2

6th-Cousins-once-removed
Theodore Seguin & Alphonsine Seguin

GEN.						GEN.
X	Jean **Mallet** m. 1618 Guillemette Ruelland	Ch.74	Ch.73	René **Hardy** m. 1686 Renée Noget		XI
IX	Ch.74	Pierre **Mallet***	m. 1662	Marie Anne **Hardy**	Ch.135	X
VIII	Louis **Mallet** m. 1697 Jeanne Brunet	Ch.10	Ch.135	Pierre Perthuis* m. 1716 M.Catherine **Mallet**		IX
VII	Pierre Seguin* m. 1739 Josephte **Mallet**	Ch.10	Ch.18	Jean-Baptiste Campeau m. 1737 Catherine **Perthuis**		VIII
VI	Jean-Louis **Seguin** m. 1779 M.Josephte Brazeau	Ch.10	Ch.18	Jean-Baptiste **Campeau** m. 1764 M.Catherine Boyer		VII
V	Jean-Baptiste **Seguin** m. 1818 M.Louise Girard	Ch.2	Ch.18	Joseph Seguin* m. 1790 Archange **Campeau**		VI
IV	Eustache **Seguin** m. 1856 Philomene Duquette	Ch.2	Ch.3	Jean-Baptiste Seguin* m. 1829 Julie Beausoleil		V
III	Napoleon **Seguin** m. 1895 Exilda Poirier	Ch.2	Ch.3	Joseph Seguin* m. 1860 Marcelline Cusson		IV
			Ch.3	Philippe Seguin* m. 1891 Delima Breault		III
II	Ch.1	Theodore **Seguin**	m. 1926	Alphonsine **Seguin***	Ch.1	II
I	Leonard Philip Antoinette Jerome Aline Roger					I

*Mallet *dit* Malichon   *Pertuhuis *dit* Lalime   *Seguin *dit* Laderoute

APPENDIX A — SUMMARY LINEAGES

APPENDIX A-3

Indigenous Ancestry

From Gisis Bahmahmaadjimiwin‡ to Theodore Seguin

Gen.	Father	Marriage	Mother	Chart
XIII	‡ unknown Nipissing man	m. ? Lake Nipissing	‡ unknown Nipissing woman	Ch.444
XII	Jean Nicolet C.1698-1742	m. ? Lake Nipissing	‡ **Gisis Bahmahmaadjimiwin** C.1602-C.1628	Ch.444
XI	Elie Dussault 1635-C.1680	m. 1663 Quebec City	**M.Madeleine Euprosine Nicolet** C.1628-1689	Ch.123
X	**Jean Francois Dussault** 1668-C.1719	m. 1692 Lauzon, Que.	M.Madeleine Bourassa 1673-1742	Ch.123
IX	Pierre Thiboutot 1687-1749	m. 1717 Lauzon, Que.	**M.Anne Dussault** 1693- ?	Ch.123
VIII	Joseph Bouchard 1706-1774	m. 1744 Ste. Anne..., Que	**M.Madeleine Thiboutot** C.1723-1772	Ch.16
VII	J.B. Charbonneau 1752-1817	m. 1770 Laval, Que.	**M.Marguerite Bouchard** C.1749-C.1783	Ch.16
VI	Francois Paquet* 1769-1846	m. 1793 Laval, Que.	Marie Charbonneau 1774-1825	Ch.16
V	**Jospeh Paquet*** 1799-C.1888	m. 1821 Laval, Que.	M.Angelique Labelle 1802-1851	Ch.2
IV	Pierre Poirier 1831-1899	m. 1877 L'Orignal, Ont.	**Martine Paquet*** **1842-1916**	Ch.2
III	George Napoleon Seguin 1870-1940	m. 1895, Thurso, Que.	**Exilda Poirier** 1877-1942	Ch.2
II	**Theodore Seguin** 1904-1979	m. 1926 Belle River, Ont.	Alphonsine Seguin* 1901-1988	Ch.1
I	Leonard Philip Antoinette Jerome Aline Roger			Ch.1

Bloodline in **BOLD** type   ‡ Indigenous person   *Paquet *dit* Bernardon   *Seguin *dit* Laderoute

APPENDIX A-4

Indigenous Ancestry

From Marie Ouchistauichkoue‡ to Alphonsine Seguin

Gen.	Father	Marriage	Mother	Chart
XII	‡ **Roch Manitouabeouich** Wendat	m. C.1625 Sillery, Que	‡ **Outchibahanoukoueou** Wabenaki or Algonquin	Ch.176 note 8
XI	Martin Prévost 1611-1691	m. 1644 Quebec City	‡ **M.Ouchistauichkoue Olivier** C.1625-1665	Ch.176
X	Michel Giroux 1661-1715	m. 1683 Beauport, Que.	**M.Therese Prévost** 1665-1743	Ch.176
IX	**Noel Giroux** 1686-1750	m. 1707 Beauport, Que.	M.Francoise Galien 1689-1754	Ch.176
VIII	**Pierre Giroux** 1712-1773	m. 1738 Beauport, Que.	M.Jeanne Toupin 1713-1762	Ch.24
VII	Francois Boucher C.1743-1819	m. 1772 Berthierville, Que.	**M.Louise Giroux** 1753-1819	Ch.24
VI	**J.B. Boucher** 1782-1857	m. 1806 Berthierville, Que.	Genevieve Dauphin 1787-1844	Ch.24
V	**Joseph Boucher** 1815-1843	m. 1841 Ste. Elisabeth, Que.	Henriette Robillard 1820-1898	Ch.3
IV	Méderic Breault 1841-1934	m. 1860 St. Jean de Matha, Que.	**M.Henriette Boucher** 1842-1901	Ch.3
III	Philippe Seguin 1866-1954	m. 1891 Tecumseh, Ont.	**Delima Breault** 1868-1946	Ch.3
II	Theodore Seguin 1904-1979	m. 1926 Belle River, Ont.	**Alphonsine Seguin*** 1901-1988	Ch.1
I	Leonard Philip Antoinette Jerome Aline Roger			Ch.1

Bloodline in **BOLD** type   ‡ Indigenous person   *Seguin *dit* Laderoute

APPENDIX A — SUMMARY LINEAGES

APPENDIX A-5

Indigenous Ancestry

From Marie Madeleine St. Jean‡ to Alphonsine Seguin

GEN.				CHART
XI	‡ unkown Onondaga man	m. ? *Iroquois territory (NY)*	‡ unknown Onondaga woman	Ch.149 note 4
X	Francois Francoeur* c.1660-1695	m. 1689 *Montreal*	‡ **M.Madeleine St. Jean** c.1672-1700	Ch.149
IX	Pierre Dumesnil* 1696-1726	m. 1716 *Quebec City*	**Marguerite Duchêne*** 1696-1758	Ch.149
VIII	Francois Moitié c.1706-1782	m. 1741 *Beauharnois, Que.*	**Marie Dumesnil*** 1723-1794	Ch.20
VII	Michel Cusson* 1744-1813	m. 1768 *Chambly, Que.*	**M.Archange Moitié** 1750-1784	Ch.20
VI	**George Cusson*** 1771-1828	m. 1800 *Chambly, Que.*	Marguerite Cognac* 1775-c.1820	Ch.20
V	**Léon Cusson** 1811-1853	m. 1837 *Sandwich, Ont.*	M.Louise Nouvion 1819-1897	Ch.3
IV	Joseph Seguin 1829-1912	m. 1860 *Tecumseh, Ont.*	**Marcelline Cusson** 1840-1931	Ch.3
III	**Philippe Seguin** 1866-1954	m. 1891 *Tecumseh, Ont.*	Delima Breault 1868-1946	Ch.3
II	Theodore Seguin 1904-1979	m. 1926 *Belle River, Ont.*	**Alphonsine Seguin*** 1901-1988	Ch.1
I	Leonard Philip Antoinette Jerome Aline Roger			Ch.1

Bloodline in **BOLD** type   ‡ Indigenous person   *Cognac *dit* Léveillé   *Cusson *dit* L'Ange
*Dumesnil *dit* Lamusique   *Francoeur *dit* Lavallée
*Seguin *dit* Laderoute

APPENDIX A-6

Indigenous Ancestry

From Jean-Baptiste Prévert‡ to Theodore Seguin

Gen.				Chart
X	‡ unknown Pawnee man	m. ? *Nebraska*	‡ unknown Pawnee woman	Ch.95
IX	‡ **J.B. Prévert** C.1680-1727	m. 1710 *Montreal*	M.Genevieve Anne Desforges* 1691-1744	Ch.95
VIII	J.B. Samson 1720-1775	m. 1746 *Quebec City*	**M.Elisabeth Prévert** 1721-1754	Ch.13
VII	**Ignace Samson** 1752-1818	m. 1781 *Quebec City*	M.Josephte Vallerand 1761-1832	Ch.13
VI	**Amable Regis Samson** 1785-1871	m. 1812 *La Prairie, Que.*	Angelique Nieding 1788-1855	Ch.13
V	Amable Duquette 1808-C.1871	m. 1832 *Chateauguay, Que.*	**Emelie Samson** 1813-1896	Ch.2
IV	Eustache Seguin 1833-1886	m. 1856 *Rigaud, Que.*	**Philomene Duquette** 1837-1889	Ch.2
III	**Napoleon Seguin** 1870-1940	m. 1895 *Thurso, Que.*	Exilda Poirier 1877-1942	Ch.2
II	**Theodore Seguin** 1904-1979	m. 1926 *Belle River, Ont.*	Alphonsine Seguin* 1901-1988	Ch.1
I	Leonard Philip Antoinette Jerome Aline Roger			Ch.1

Bloodline in **BOLD** type   ‡ Indigenous person   *Desforges *dit* St. Maurice   *Seguin *dit* Laderoute

APPENDIX A-7

Indigenous Ancestry

From Nicolas Doyon‡ to Alphonsine Seguin

GEN.				CHART
XI	‡ unknown Pawnee man	m. ? Nebraska	‡unknown Pawnee woman	Ch.157
X	**Nicolas Doyon*** C.1684-1727	m. 1710 Boucherville, Que.	M.Louise Gareau 1688-1769	Ch.157
IX	Pierre Veronneau* 1704-1773	m. 1730 Boucherville, Que.	**M.Josephte Doyon*** 1713-1739	Ch.157
VIII	Joseph Amable Delières 1730-1806	m. 1759 Boucherville, Que.	**Veronique Veronneau*** 1736-1773	Ch.21
VII	Pierre Letourneau 1744-1818	m. 1784 Detroit	**Louise Delières** 1765-1832	Ch.21
VI	Joseph Nouvion* 1774-1828	m. 1808 Sandwich, Ont.	**Angelique Letourneau** 1791-1843	Ch.21
V	Léon Cusson 1811-1853	m. 1837 Sandwich, Ont.	**M.Louise Nouvion*** 1819-1897	Ch.3
IV	Joseph Seguin 1829-1912	m. 1860 Tecumseh, Ont.	**Marcelline Cusson** 1840-1931	Ch.3
III	**Philippe Seguin** 1866-1854	m. 1891 Tecumseh, Ont.	Delima Breault 1868-1946	Ch.3
II	Theodore Seguin 1904-1979	m. 1926 Belle River, Ont.	**Alphonsine Seguin*** 1901-1988	Ch.1
I	Leonard Philip Antoinette Jerome Aline Roger			Ch.1

(Bloodline in **BOLD** type)   ‡ Indigenous person   *Doyon *dit* Laframboise   *Nouvion *dit* Sanscartier
*Seguin *dit* Laderoute   *Veronneau *dit* Denis

Appendix A-8

The First European Child (1)

From Hélène Desportes & Guillaume Hébert to Alphonsine Seguin

Gen.				
XII	Louis Hébert m. 1601 Marie Rolet		Pierre Desportes m. C.1619 Francoise Langlois	Ch.463
XI	Guillaume Hébert C.1614-1639	m. 1634 Quebec City	**Hélène Desportes** C.1620-1675	Ch.141
X	Guillaume Fournier C.1623-1699	m. 1651 Quebec City	**Francoise Hébert** 1638-1716	Ch.141
IX	Jacques Boulet 1664-1738	m.1686 Montmagny, Que.	**M.Francoise Fournier** 1671-1734	Ch.141
VIII	Pierre Morin 1683-1767	m. 1707 Montmagny, Que.	**M.Francoise Boulet** C.1687-1764	Ch.19
VII	Joseph Malboeuf* C.1725-1801	m. 1750, St. Pierre, Que.	**M.Reine Morin** C.1732-1813	Ch.19
VI	**Augustin Malboeuf*** 1759-1812	m. 1784 St. Eustache, Que.	Monique Bouchard 1763-1844	Ch.19
V	Jean-Baptiste Seguin 1798-1871	m. 1829 Detroit	**Julie Beausoleil*** 1807-1890	Ch.3
IV	**Joseph Seguin** 1829-1912	m. 1860 Tecumseh, Ont.	Marcelline Cusson 1840-1931	Ch.3
III	**Philippe Seguin*** 1866-1954	m. 1891 Tecumseh, Ont.	Delima Breault 1868-1946	Ch.3
II	Theodore Seguin 1904-1979	m. 1926 Belle River, Ont.	**Alphonsine Seguin*** 1901-1988	Ch.1
I	**Leonard Philip Antoinette Jerome Aline Roger**			Ch.1

Bloodline in **BOLD** type   *Malboeuf *dit* Beausoleil   *Seguin *dit* Laderoute

APPENDIX A — SUMMARY LINEAGES

APPENDIX A-9

The First European Child (2)

From Hélène Desportes & Noel Morin to Alphonsine Seguin

Gen.	Father	Marriage	Mother	Ref.
XIII	Claude Morin m. C.1615 Jeanne Moreau		Pierre Desportes m. C.1619 Francoise Langlois	Ch.491
XII	Noel Morin C.1616-1680	m. 1640 Quebec City	**Hélène Desportes** C.1620-1675	Ch.491
XI	Nicolas Gaudry C.1620-1669	m. 1653 Quebec City	**Agnes Morin** 1641-1687	Ch.168
X	Jean Hamel 1651-1711	m. 1677 Que.	**M.Charlotte Christine Gaudry** 1660-1729	Ch.168
IX	**Charles Hamel** 1679-1755	m. 1701 Que.	M.Angelique Gauthier 1682-1732	Ch168.
VIII	**Jean-Baptiste Hamel** 1710-1770	m. 1735 Vercheres, Que.	M.Catherine Vegiard C.1713-1809	Ch.23
VII	Louis Prisque Roberge* 1752-1813	m. 1773 St. Sulpice, Que.	**M.Josephte Hamel** 1756-1842	Ch.23
VI	**Louis Roberge*** C.1773-1840	m. 1800 Repentigny, Que.	Angelique Morisseau 1781-1827	Ch.23
V	Jeremie Brault 1808-1884	m. 1829 St. Sulpice, Que.	**Zoe Roberge*** 1811-1884	Ch.3
IV	**Méderic Breault** 1841-1934	m. 1860 St Jean de Matha, Que.	M.Henriette Boucher 1842-1901	Ch.3
III	Philippe Seguin* 1866-1954	m. 1891 Tecumseh, Ont.	**Delima Breault** 1868-1946	Ch.3
II	Theodore Seguin 1904-1979	m. 1926 Belle River, Ont.	**Alphonsine Seguin*** 1901-1988	Ch.1
I	Leonard Philip **Antoinette** Jerome Aline Roger			Ch.1

Bloodline in **BOLD** type   *Roberge *dit* Lacroix   *Seguin *dit* Laderoute

APPENDIX A-10

The Plains of Abraham

From Abraham Martin to Alphonsine Seguin

GEN.				
XII	Abraham Martin* C.1589-1664	m. 1615 Dieppe, France	Marguerite Langlois C.1602-1775	Ch.456
XI	Etienne Racine C.1605-1689	m. 1638 Quebec City	**Marguerite Martin** 1624-1679	Ch.133
X	Noel Simard C.1637-1715	m.1661 Chateau Richer, Que.	**M.Madeleine Racine** 1646-1726	Ch.133
IX	**Francois Simard** 1678-1732	m. 1712 Que.	Ursule Paré 1689-1759	Ch.133
VIII	Pierre Tremblay 1708-1763	m. 1734 Les Eboulements, Que.	**Madeleine Simard** 1713-1750	Ch.18
VII	Joseph Seguin* 1717-1795	m. 1751 Detroit	**M.Therese Tremblay** 1734-1800	Ch18.
VI	**Joseph Seguin*** 1764-1839	m. 1790 Detroit	Archange Campeau 1771-1822	Ch.18
V	**Jean-Baptiste Seguin*** 1798-1871	m. 1829 Sandwich, Ont.	Julie Beausoleil* 1807-1890	Ch.3
IV	**Joseph Seguin*** 1829-1912	m. 1860 Tecumseh, Ont.	Marcelline Cusson 1840-1931	Ch.3
III	**Philippe Seguin*** 1866-1954	m. 1891 Tecumseh, Ont.	Delima Breault 1868-1946	Ch.3
II	Theodore Seguin 1904-1979	m. 1926 Belle River, Ont.	**Alphonsine Seguin*** 1901-1988	Ch.1
I	Leonard Philip Antoinette Jerome Aline Roger			Ch.1

Bloodline in **BOLD** type   *Martin *dit* L'Écossais   *Malboeuf *dit* Beausoleil   *Seguin *dit* Laderoute

APPENDIX A — SUMMARY LINEAGES

APPENDIX A-11

A Founder of Montreal

From Léonard Lucos to Theodore Seguin

GEN.				
XI	**Leonard Lucos*** 1626-1651	m. 1648 Montreal	Barbe Poisson C.1633-1722	Ch.109
X	René Cuillerier* 1637-1713	m. 1665 Montreal	**Marie Lucos** 1650-1727	Ch.109
IX	**René Cuillerier** 1690-1771	m. 1710 Cap Santé, Que	M.Jeanne Anne Corneau 1694-1756	Ch.109
VIII	Michel Deschamps* 1722-1792	m. 1742 Ste. Anne, Que.	**M.Charlotte Cuillerier** 1725- ?	Ch.15
VII	**Pierre Deschamps** 1751-1826	m. 1779 Vaudreuil, Que.	M.Angelique Daoust 1760-1797	Ch.15
VI	**Pierre Deschamps** C.1782-1839	m. 1804 Vaudreuil, Que.	Archange Dufort 1789-1846	Ch.15
V	Jean-Baptiste Poirier 1802-1875	m. 1827 Vaudreuil, Que.	**Josephte Deschamps** 1809- ?	Ch.2
IV	**Pierre Poirier** 1831-1899	m. 1877 L'Orignal, Ont.	Martine Paquet* 1842-1916	Ch.2
III	Napoleon Seguin 1870-1940	m. 1895 Thurso, Que.	**Exilda Poirier** 1877-1942	Ch.2
II	**Theodore Seguin** 1904-1979	m. 1926 Belle River, Ont.	Alphonsine Seguin* 1901-1988	Ch.1
I	Leonard Philip Antoinette Jerome Aline Roger			Ch.1

*Cuillerier *dit* Léveillé   *Hunault *dit* Deschamps   *Lucos *dit* Barbot   Paquet *dit* Bernardon   *Seguin *dit* Laderoute

Appendix A-12

A German Soldier in America

From Gebhardt Nieding to Theodore Seguin

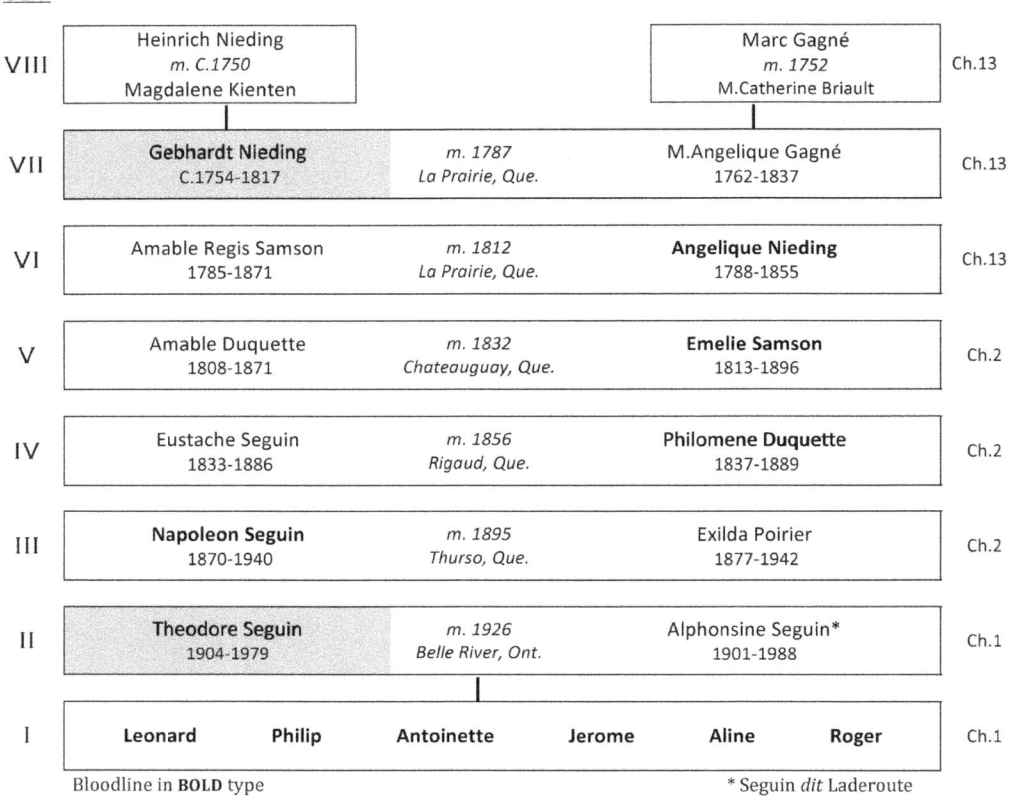

GEN.				
VIII	Heinrich Nieding *m. C.1750* Magdalene Kienten		Marc Gagné *m. 1752* M.Catherine Briault	Ch.13
VII	**Gebhardt Nieding** C.1754-1817	*m. 1787* *La Prairie, Que.*	M.Angelique Gagné 1762-1837	Ch.13
VI	Amable Regis Samson 1785-1871	*m. 1812* *La Prairie, Que.*	**Angelique Nieding** 1788-1855	Ch.13
V	Amable Duquette 1808-1871	*m. 1832* *Chateauguay, Que.*	**Emelie Samson** 1813-1896	Ch.2
IV	Eustache Seguin 1833-1886	*m. 1856* *Rigaud, Que.*	**Philomene Duquette** 1837-1889	Ch.2
III	**Napoleon Seguin** 1870-1940	*m. 1895* *Thurso, Que.*	Exilda Poirier 1877-1942	Ch.2
II	**Theodore Seguin** 1904-1979	*m. 1926* *Belle River, Ont.*	Alphonsine Seguin* 1901-1988	Ch.1
I	**Leonard Philip Antoinette Jerome Aline Roger**			Ch.1

Bloodline in **BOLD** type   * Seguin *dit* Laderoute

APPENDIX A — SUMMARY LINEAGES

APPENDIX A-13

A Captive and 11th Cousins?

Marc Seguin & Marjorie Cluett

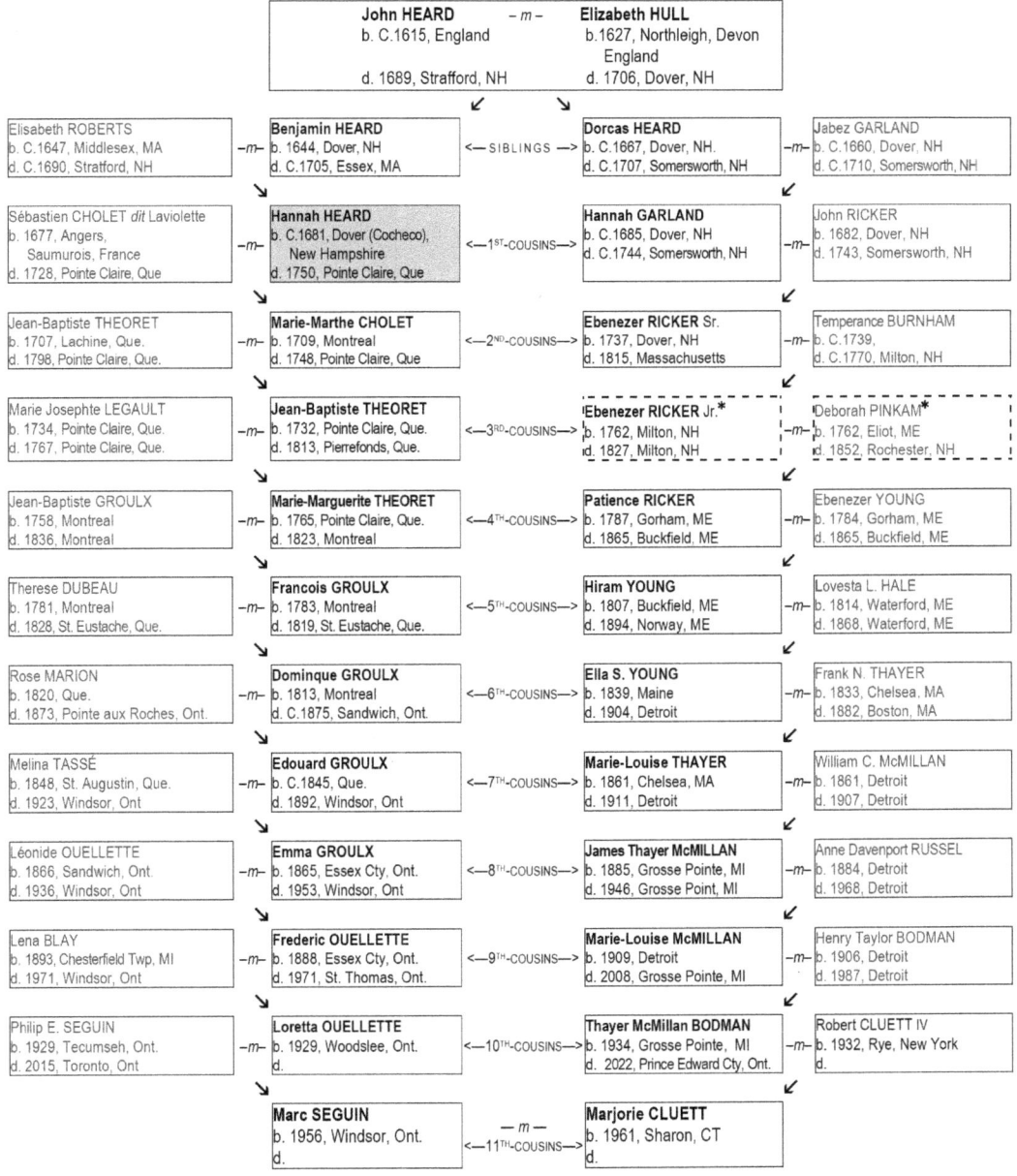

* Further research is required to confirm this link in the lineage.

Appendix A-14

A Deerfield Captive
From Sarah Allen to Theodore Seguin

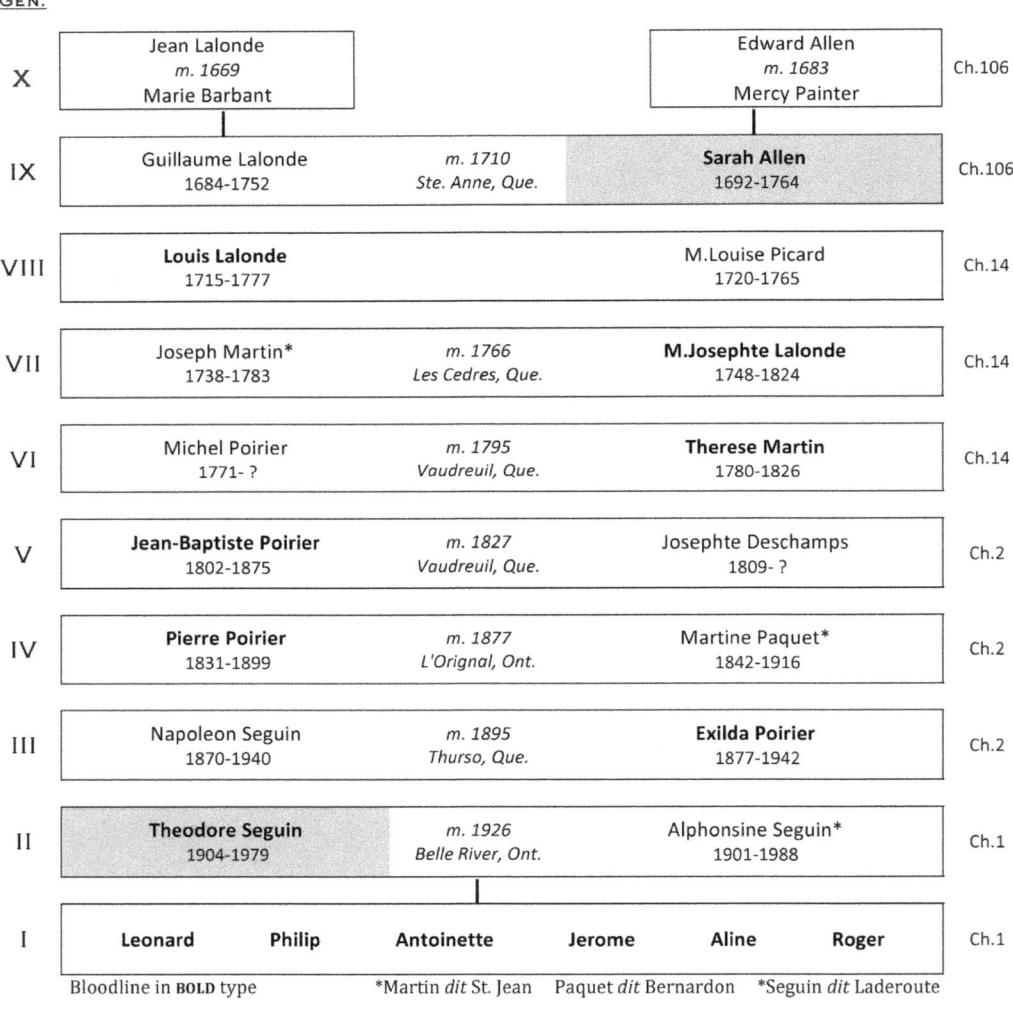

APPENDIX A-15

Twice Captured by the Iroquois
From Michel Messier to Alphonsine Seguin

Gen.				
XI	**Michel Messier*** C.1641-1725	m. 1658 Montreal	Anne Lemoine 1638-1725	Ch.153
X	Jean-Baptiste Brodeur* 1653-1718	m. 1679 Boucherville, Que.	**M.Anne Messier** 1665-1751	Ch.153
IX	Paul Bissonnet 1690-1723	m. 1712, Varennes, Que.	**M.Anne Brodeur** 1692-1753	Ch.153
VIII	Jacques Lavigne* 1701-1755	m. 1729 Varennes, Que.	**M.Anne Bissonnet** 1712-1791	Ch.21
VII	Jacques Nouvion 1736-1781	m. 1760 Varennes, Que.	**M.Anne Lavigne** 1737-1804	Ch.21
VI	**Joseph Nouvion** 1774-1828	m. 1808 Sandwich, Ont.	Angelique Letourneau 1791-1843	Ch.21
V	Léon Cusson 1811-1853	m. 1837 Sandwich, Ont.	**M.Louise Nouvion** 1819-1897	Ch.3
IV	Joseph Seguin* 1829-1912	m. 1860 Tecumseh, Ont.	**Marcelline Cusson** 1840-1931	Ch.3
III	**Philippe Seguin*** 1866-1954	m. 1891 Tecumseh, Ont.	Delima Breault 1868-1946	Ch.3
II	Theodore Seguin 1904-1979	m. 1926 Belle River, Ont.	**Alphonsine Seguin*** 1901-1988	Ch.1
I	Leonard Philip Antoinette Jerome Aline Roger			Ch.1

*Brodeur *dit* Lavigne   Lavigne *dit* Brisetout   *Messier *dit* St. Michel   Nouvion *dit* Sanscartier   *Seguin *dit* Laderoute

APPENDIX A-16

Settlers at Detroit (1)

From Pierre Mallet to Alphonsine Seguin

Gen.				
XI	Pierre Mallet m. 1662 M.Anne Hardy		Felix Tuné* m. 1665 Elisabeth Lefebvre	Ch.135
X	**Pierre Mallet** 1676-1739	m. 1698 Montreal	M.Madeleine Tuné* 1673-1739	Ch.135
IX	Pierre Perthuis* 1691-1758	m. 1716 Montreal	**M.Catherine Mallet** 1698-1745	Ch.135
VIII	Jean-Baptiste Campeau 1711-1783	m. 1737 Detroit	**Catherine Perthuis*** 1718-1763	Ch.18
VII	**Jean-Baptiste Campeau** 1737-1798	m. 1764 Detroit	M.Catherine Boyer 1746-1814	Ch.18
VI	Joseph Seguin* 1764-1839	m. 1790 Detroit	**Archange Campeau** 1771-1822	Ch.18
V	**Jean-Baptiste Seguin*** 1798-1871	m. 1829 Sandwich, Ont.	Julie Beausoleil* 1807-1890	Ch.3
IV	**Joseph Seguin*** 1829-1912	m. 1860 Tecumseh, Ont.	Marcelline Cusson 1840-1931	Ch.3
III	**Philippe Seguin*** 1866-1954	m. 1891 Tecumseh, Ont.	Delima Breault 1868-1946	Ch.3
II	Theodore Seguin 1904-1979	m. 1926 Belle River, Ont.	**Alphonsine Seguin*** 1901-1988	Ch.1
I	Leonard Philip Antoinette Jerome Aline Roger			Ch.1

Bloodline in **BOLD** type   *Perthuis *dit* Lalime   *Seguin *dit* Laderoute   *Tuné *dit* Dufresne

APPENDIX A – SUMMARY LINEAGES

APPENDIX A-17

Settlers at Detroit (2)

From René Daigneau to Theodore Seguin

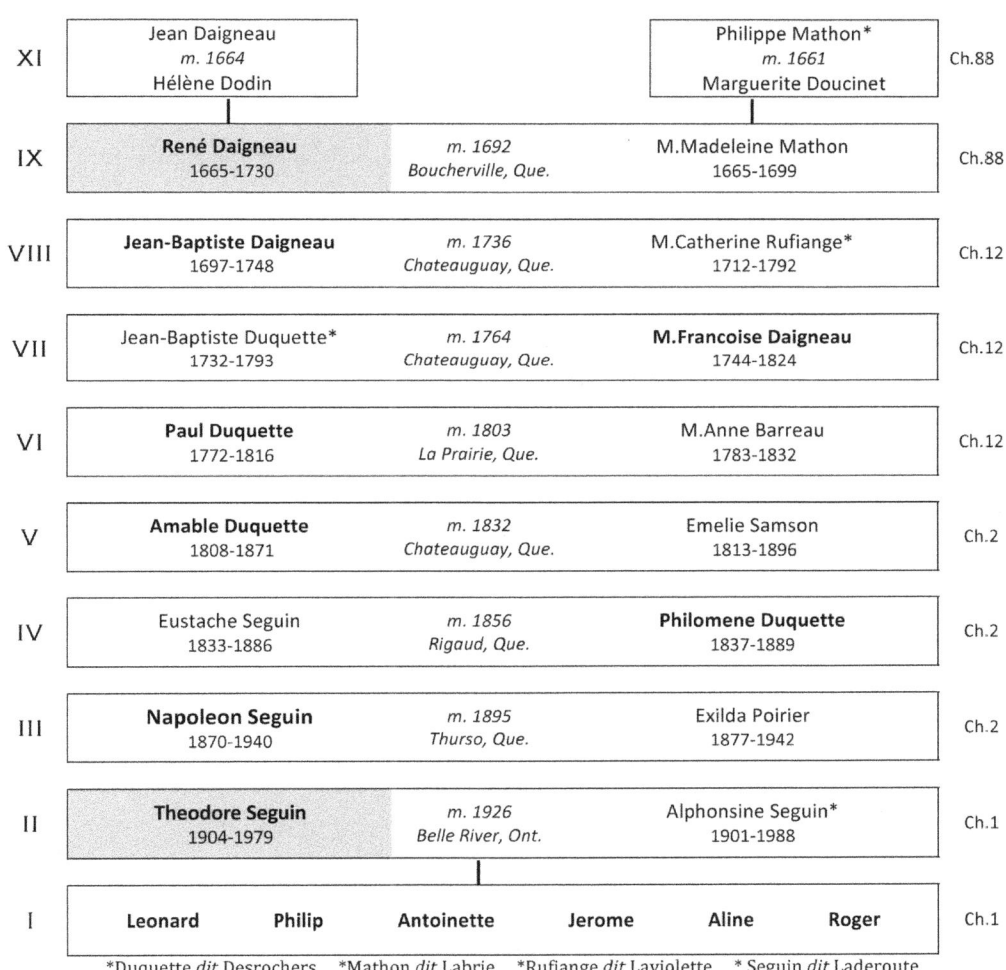

GEN.				
XI	Jean Daigneau m. 1664 Hélène Dodin		Philippe Mathon* m. 1661 Marguerite Doucinet	Ch.88
IX	**René Daigneau** 1665-1730	m. 1692 *Boucherville, Que.*	M.Madeleine Mathon 1665-1699	Ch.88
VIII	**Jean-Baptiste Daigneau** 1697-1748	m. 1736 *Chateauguay, Que.*	M.Catherine Rufiange* 1712-1792	Ch.12
VII	Jean-Baptiste Duquette* 1732-1793	m. 1764 *Chateauguay, Que.*	**M.Francoise Daigneau** 1744-1824	Ch.12
VI	**Paul Duquette** 1772-1816	m. 1803 *La Prairie, Que.*	M.Anne Barreau 1783-1832	Ch.12
V	**Amable Duquette** 1808-1871	m. 1832 *Chateauguay, Que.*	Emelie Samson 1813-1896	Ch.2
IV	Eustache Seguin 1833-1886	m. 1856 *Rigaud, Que.*	**Philomene Duquette** 1837-1889	Ch.2
III	**Napoleon Seguin** 1870-1940	m. 1895 *Thurso, Que.*	Exilda Poirier 1877-1942	Ch.2
II	**Theodore Seguin** 1904-1979	m. 1926 *Belle River, Ont.*	Alphonsine Seguin* 1901-1988	Ch.1
I	Leonard Philip Antoinette Jerome Aline Roger			Ch.1

*Duquette *dit* Desrochers   *Mathon *dit* Labrie   *Rufiange *dit* Laviolette   * Seguin *dit* Laderoute

Appendix A-18

3rd-Cousin to Her Mother-in-Law

Loretta Ouellette and Alphonsine Seguin

Gen.							Gen.
VI	Joseph Seguin* m. 1751 M.Therese Tremblay	Ch.18		Ch.18	Jean-Baptiste Campeau m. 1764 M.Catherine Boyer		VI
VI	Ch.18	**Joseph Seguin***	m. 1790	**Archange Campeau**	Ch.18		V
V	**Jean-Baptiste Seguin*** m. 1829 Julie Beausoleil	Ch.3		Ch.5	Jean-Baptiste Lauzon m. 1828 **Euphrosine Seguin***		IV
IV	Joseph Seguin m. 1860 Marcelline Cusson	Ch.3		Ch.5	Joseph Blay m. 1866 **Archange Lauzon**		III
III	Philippe Seguin m. 1891 Delima Breault	Ch.3		Ch.5	Frederic Ouellette m. 1910 **Lena Blay**		II
II	Theodore Seguin m. 1926 **Alphonsine Seguin***	Ch.1		Ch.1	**Loretta Ouellette**		I
I	Ch.1	**Philip Seguin**	m. 1953				
		Randall A.	Marc P.	Daniel E.	Laurel T.		

* Seguin *dit* Laderoute

APPENDIX A-19

3rd-Cousins-once-removed

Eustache Seguin & Philomene Duquette

Gen.					Gen.
IX	Pierre **Mallet** m. 1662 M.Anne Hardy	Ch.74	Ch.75	Francois **Brunet*** m. 1672 Barbe Beauvais*	X
VIII	**Louis Mallet** m. 1697 Jeanne **Brunet***			Ch.10	IX
VII	Pierre Seguin* m. 1739 M.Josephte **Mallet**	Ch.10	Ch.12	Charles Duquette m. 1719 M.Catherine **Mallet**	VIII
			Ch.12	**J.B. Duquette** m. 1764 M.Francoise Daigneau	VII
VI	Jean-Louis **Seguin*** m. 1779 M.Josephte Brazeau	Ch.10	Ch.12	Paul **Duquette** m. 1803 M.Anne Barreau	VI
V	Jean-Baptiste **Seguin*** m. 1818 M.Louise Girard	Ch.2	Ch.2	Amable **Duquette** m. 1832 Emelie Samson	V
IV	**Eustache Seguin** m. 1856 **Philomene Duquette**			Ch.2	IV
III		Napoleon Seguin m. 1895 Exilda Poirier	Ch.2		III
II		Theodore Seguin m. 1926 Alphonsine Seguin	Ch.1		II
I	Leonard Philip Antoinette Jerome Aline Roger				I

* Beauvais *dit* St. Gemme   * Brunet *dit* Bourbonnais   * Seguin *dit* Laderoute

Appendix B

François Seguin's Arrival in Canada

It is widely accepted by many historians, both amateur and professional, that Francois SEGUIN *dit* Laderoute, was a soldier in the Carignan-Salières regiment which arrived in Canada in 1665 [see Verney, Fournier & Langlois, and Gagné "Cy Devant"]. However, historians who have examined the source documents concerning the regiment have yet to find an original nominal roll listing all of the names of the soldiers. One later list of more than 400 names of those soldiers of the regiment who settled in Canada does not include Francois SEGUIN *dit* Laderoute. [LAC, MG1-D2C, Microfilm reel number: C-9149, F-582] It is generally acknowledged that this list is incomplete and many other key documents concerning the Carignan-Salières regiment have never come to light.

While it is most likely that Francois was a soldier in the regiment, and that he arrived with the Saint-Ours company aboard the ship *La Justice* in September, 1665, known lists of passengers aboard this ship do not include the name Seguin or Laderoute. However, the nominal strength of the company was fifty men plus officers, and only thirty-eight names appear on the passenger list for *La Justice* in 1665. [https://www.geni.com/projects/Passagers-du-Justice-1665/25445]

The idea that Francois SEGUIN *dit* Laderoute arrived in Canada with the Carignan-Salières regiment is based largely on the later actions of the company commander, Pierre de Saint-Ours, who, in 1672, was granted an enormous tract of land — a seigneury — on the banks of the Richelieu River. At that time, Saint-Ours needed to populate his seigneury with *censitaires* — tenants who would be granted land by him and which they would have to clear and cultivate. A portion of the harvests from these farms would go to the seigneur to provide him with an income. A number of soldiers who had served under Saint-Ours were granted land on his seigneury. Francois Seguin was also granted land on the Saint-Ours seigneury. In addition, near the end of his life, the seigneur included a number of his soldiers' names in his will. Fifty *livres* were to go to the heirs of Francois Seguin. [Couillard-Despres, p.96]

Taken together, the land grant on the Saint-Ours seigneury and the inheritance are strong evidence that Francois SEGUIN had, indeed, served under Captain Saint-Ours. However, this service may not have been as a soldier in the Carignan-Salières regiment.

In 1669, a contingent of more than 300 ex-soldiers arrived in New France. [Eccles, *Canada*, p.47] In exchange for helping to settle in the colony, these men were promised land of their own — something most of them could never hope for if they stayed in France. A number of these newly-arrived soldiers joined the Montreal (Ville Marie) garrison which protected the town in the event of further Iroquois attacks. Francois SEGUIN was part of this defence force, and Pierre de Saint-Ours had been appointed commander of the Montreal garrison.

So, Francois SEGUIN *dit* Laderoute may have arrived in Canada in 1669 and then gone on to serve in the Montreal garrison under Captain Saint-Ours. Without solid documentary evidence either way, we may never know if he arrived in Canada as an ex-soldier in 1669, or with the Carignan-Salières regiment in 1665. We do know that, at some point, Pierre de Saint-Ours was his commanding officer. We also know that, at Boucherville, Que. in 1672, Francois married the *fille du Roi,* Jeanne PETIT, and that their offspring were the progenitors of an enormous number of Seguin descendants.

Other references:
  www.fichierorigine.com/recherche?nom=&commune=&pays=&mariagerech=&regiment=1
  https://fillesduroi.org/cpage.php?pt=12
  www.geni.com/projects/Passagers-pour-la-Nouvelle-France-1534-1763/24655

Appendix C

A War of 1812 Research Project

During the course of the War of 1812 (1812-1814), several direct ancestors of Theodore Seguin and Alphonsine Seguin would have been between the ages of 16 and 60, making them eligible for military service.

When war broke out between the United States and Great Britain in June, 1812, Canada became the main battleground. In July of that year, the American Army under General William Hull occupied the town of Sandwich, Ont., but retreated back across the Detroit river four weeks later. In August, Major-General Isaac Brock led the British Army along with the Canadian militia and their Indigenous allies attacked Detroit. Fearing a massacre by the native warriors, Hull surrendered Fort Detroit, and the British occupied the town and fort until September, 1813.

Alphonsine's 2nd-great-grandfather, Joseph SEGUIN *dit* Laderoute (b.1764) (Ch.18-2), would have been 48 years old at the time of the American surrender. It is unclear whether or not he was still living on the American side of the border or if he had already moved across the river to Sandwich Township in Upper Canada. Either way, Joseph would have been eligible to serve either in the American militia or in the Canadian militia, depending on where his loyalties lay. Before the war ended in 1814, Joseph's son, Jean-Baptiste (Ch.3-14), would have been 16 years old and he, too, may have been called on to fight for one side or another. In addition, another of Alphonsine's 2nd-great-grandfathers who was the living in Sandwich when war broke out would also have been eligible to serve in the Upper Canada militia. This was Joseph NOUVION (Ch.21-2), himself the son of a soldier who had served in the French Army's Béarn Regiment in Canada more than fifty years earlier.

On the Montreal front, the militia in Lower Canada was embodied shortly after the commencement of the war. In 1813, an attempt by the American Army to capture Montreal ended in their defeat at the Battle of Chateauguay. No fewer than twelve direct Seguin ancestors living in the Montreal region at the time would have been of age to be eligible for military service:

> Antoine BRAULT *dit* Lafleur (Ch.22-2), age 43, Alphonsine's 2nd-great-grandfather
> George CUSSON *dit* L'Ange (Ch.20-2), age 41, Alphonsine's 2nd-great-grandfather
> J.B. DUFORT *dit* Lacouture (Ch.15-6), age 46, Theodore's 3rd-great-grandfather
> Paul DUQUETTE *dit* Desrochers (Ch.12-2), age 40, Theodore's 2nd-great-grandfather

Francois GIRARD (Ch.11-2), age 52, Theodore's 2nd-great-grandfather

Louis MORISSEAU (Ch.23-6), age 58, Alphonsine's 3rd-great-grandfather

Michel POIRIER *dit* Desloge (Ch.14-2), age 41, Theodore's 2nd-great-grandfather

Louis ROBERGE *dit* Lacroix (Ch.23-2), age 39, Alphonsine's 2nd-great-grandfather

Antoine ROBILLARD *dit* Lambert (Ch.25-2), age 22, Alphonsine's 2nd-great-grandfather

Amable Regis SAMSON (Ch.13-2), age 27, Theodore's 2nd-great-grandfather

Jean-Baptiste SEGUIN (Ch.2-8), age 16 (in 1813), Theodore's 1st-great-grandfather

Jean-Louis SEGUIN *dit* Laderoute (Ch.10-2), age 59, Theodore's 2nd-great-grandfather.

Further research is required to determine if any of these men in the Detroit River region or in the Montreal area were called to serve in the local militia companies or other military units during the War of 1812.

Appendix D
List of *dit* Names

Many of the more than 200 different *dit* names used by the ancestors of Theodore Seguin and Alphonsine Seguin are listed here.

Sorted by Surname

Surname	*dit* Name
AMIOT/AMYOT	Villeneuve
AUDIAU/HODIAU	Laflèche
AUNEAU	Aunois
AVERTY	Leger
BADAILLAC/BADAYAC	Laplante
BADEL	Lamarche
BANLIER	Laperle
BARBANT	Balan
BARBARY	Grandmaison
BARBE	Abel/Labelle
BARBEAU	Boisdoré
BARBEAU	Potvin
BARIL	Gobeil
BARITEAU	Lamarche
BARSA	Lafleur
BAZINET	Tourblanche
BEAR	Barbe
BEAUCHAMP	Le Grand Beauchamp
BEAUDOIN	Petit Jean
BEAULNE	Lafranchise
BEAUMONT	Rat
BEAUVAIS	St. Gemme
BELANGER	Catherine
BELANGER	Simoneau
BENARD	Beausoleil
BENOIT	Livernois/Nivernais
BERIAU	Potvin
BIROLEAU	Lafleur
BISSONNET	Deschaumaux
BLANCHON	Larose
BLOUIN	Belair
BLOUIN	Fortier
BOISDON	Bressart
BONHOMME	Beaupré
BONIN	Morin
BONIN	St. Martin
BONNEAU	Lemaitre
BONNIER	Laplante
BONVOULOIR	Delièrre
BOUCHARD	Lavallée
BOUCHER	Barbel
BOUCHER	Vindespagne

Sorted by *dit* Name

Surname	*dit* Name
BARBE	Abel/Labelle
PELLETIER	Antaya
LOPS	Aubert
AUNEAU	Aunois
BARBANT	Balan
BEAR	Barbe
BOUCHER	Barbel
LUCOS/LUCAULT	Barbot
PETIT	Beauchemin
DESMARAIS	Beaulac
BONHOMME	Beaupré
JARED	Beauregard
TETU	Beauregard
BENARD	Beausoleil
MALBOEUF	Beausoleil
BLOUIN	Belair
DALPÉ	Belair
DELPECHE	Belair
CHEVREFILS	Belisle
PAQUET	Bernardon
BARBEAU	Boisdoré
DENOYON	Boisdoré
GAUTHIER	Boisverdun
DELIÈRES	Bonvouloir
GRANDMAISON	Borry
LESCARBEAU	Bosseron
BRUNET	Bourbonnais
GAUDRY	Bourbonnière
DENEVERS	Brantigny
DUCHENE	Bredel
BOISDON	Bressart
LAVIGNE	Brisetout
GADOURY	Brisset
CONTENT	Bury
LESIEUR	Calot
BOULARD	Cambray
HENAULT	Canada
LEROUX	Cardinal
JAMME	Carrière
BELANGER	Catherine
CLEMENT	Chambly
PRESSEAU	Chambly

Appendix D – dit Names

Surname	dit Name
BOULARD	Cambray
BOURGEOIS	Picard
BOURGNEUF	Lafreniere
BOUTET	St. Martin
BOUTIN	Larose
BOYER	Fontaine/Lafontaine
BRAULT	Lafleur
BRIEN	Desrochers
BRIEN	Villebrillan
BRISSON	Laroche
BRODEUR	Lavigne
BRUNET	Bourbonnais
BRUNET	Létang
CAMBIN	Larivière
CARBONNEAU	Provençal
CARPENETIER	Lapierre
CARREAU	Lafraicheur
CAUCHON	Lamothe
CHAPEAU	Laframboise
CHARBONNIER	Lafleur
CHARRIER	Lafontaine
CHARRON	Ducharme
CHASLE	Duhamel
CHAUVIN	Lafortune
CHERLOT	Desmoulins
CHEVREFILS	Belisle
CLEMENT	Chambly
CLEMENT	Larivière
COGNAC	Léveillé
COITOU	St. Jean
CONTENT	Bury
CORBEIL	Tranchemontagne
COTIN	Dugal
CUILLERIER	Léveillé
CUSSON	L'Ange
DALPÉ	Belair
DAMANCOUR	Lacaille
DAMOURS	Lefret
DARAGON	Lafrance
DARVEAU	Langoumois
DASSILVA	Portugais
DEBORD	Lajeunesse
DEBOURNELLE	Chevalier
DECELLES	Duclos
DECHAUX	Latourneuse
DELIÈRES	Bonvouloir
DELPECHE	Belair
DENAULT	Lamartinière
DENEVERS	Brantigny
DENOYON	Boisdoré
DEPOITIERS	Dubuisson
LAURENT	Champagne
DESJARDINS	Charbonnier
GODIN	Chatillon
MIGNAULT	Chatillon
FLOUL	Chetouse
DEBOURNELLE	Chevalier
VALLIÈRE	Chevalier
GUILLET	Cinqmars/St. Marc
EMERY	Codère
GLADU	Cognac
GILBERT	Comtois
JUILLET	d'Avignon
DRAGON	Daragon
LEGARDEUR	Darpentigny
BONVOULOIR	Delièrre
POIRIER	Deloge/Desloge
HUBOUX	Delonchamp/Delongchamps
VERONNEAU	Denis
LARUE	Deplaine
GIRARD/GIRARDIN	Deraine
PEPIN	Descardonnets
HUNAULT/HENAULT	Deschamps
PINEAU	Deschatele
BISSONNET	Deschaumaux
MAHEU	Deshasards
FAVREAU	Deslaurier
CHERLOT	Desmoulins
MONCIAU	Desormeaux
BRIEN	Desrochers
DUQUETTE	Desrochers
MAILLOUX	Desruisseau
GAGNÉ	Dobigeon
ST. GODARD	Duboct
DEPOITIERS	Dubuisson
GUYON	Dubuisson
CHARRON	Ducharme
DECELLES	Duclos
TUNÉ	Dufresne
COTIN	Dugal
CHASLE	Duhamel
MILLOY	Dumaine
ROBINEAU	Dumoulin
GUYON	Durouvray
DRAGON	Ecayer
DRAGON	Ethier
FAILLÉ	Fayette/Lafayette
LEFEBVRE	Fevre
LESIEGE	Fontaine
BOYER	Fontaine/Lafontaine
MENARD	Fontaine/Lafontaine
BLOUIN	Fortier...

Surname	*dit* Name
DESEVE	Potvin
DESFORGES	St. Maurice
DESHAIES	St. Cyr
DESJARDINS	Charbonnier
DESJARDINS	Zacharie
DESMARAIS	Beaulac
DESOISMAISONS	Picard
DOYON	Laframboise
DRAGON	Daragon
DRAGON	Ecayer
DRAGON	Ethier
DROUSSON	Robert
DUCHENE	Bredel
DUCHENY	Lavallée
DUFORT	Lacouture
DUHAMEL	Sansfaçon
DUMAS	Rencontre
DUMESNIL	Lamusique
DUPUIS	Parisien
DUQUETTE	Desrochers
DUSSAULT	Lafleur
EMERY	Codère
ERODEAU	Larose
ESTEVE	Lajeunesse
FAILLÉ	Fayette/Lafayette
FAVREAU	Deslaurier
FEVRIER	Lacroix
FISSIAU	Laramée
FLOUL	Chetoulse
FOUCHER	St. Aubin
FRANCOEUR	Lavallée
GADOURY	Brisset
GAGNÉ	Dobigeon
GARMAN	Picard/Le Picard
GARNIER	Laforge
GAUDRY	Bourbonnière
GAUTHIER	Boisverdun
GAUTHIER	Landreville
GAUTHIER	Saguingorra
GEORGET	Tranquille
GIASSON	Lavallée
GILBERT	Comtois
GILBERT	Laframboise
GILBERT	Sanspeur
GIRARD/GIRARDIN	Deraine
GIRARDIN	Sansoucy
GLADU	Cognac
GODIN	Chatillon
GOYAU	Lagarde
GRANDMAISON	Borry
GRENIER	Nadeau

Surname	*dit* Name
OTIS	Fortier
MONTREUIL	Francoeur
BARIL	Gobeil
GUILBAULT	Grandbois
BARBARY	Grandmaison
GUITAUT	Jolicoeur
JAUFFRAY	Jolicoeur
CUSSON	L'Ange
MARTIN	L'Écossais
LAURARÉE	L'Orange
MAROTTE	Labonté
VEGIARD	Labonté
MATHON	Labrie
DAMANCOUR	Lacaille
PEPIN	Lachance
JANOT	Lachapelle
LEFEBVRE	Laciseray
DUFORT	Lacouture
FEVRIER	Lacroix
LANGEVIN	Lacroix
ROBERGE	Lacroix
SEGUIN	Laderoute
AUDIAU/HODIAU	Laflèche
RICHER	Laflèche
BARSA	Lafleur
BIROLEAU	Lafleur
BRAULT	Lafleur
CHARBONNIER	Lafleur
DUSSAULT	Lafleur
PERRIER	Lafleur
PINSONNAULT	Lafleur
POIRIER	Lafleur
SIRET	Lafleur
MOITIÉ	Lafonderie
CHARRIER	Lafontaine
GUERIN	Lafontaine
LORET	Lafontaine
PERRAS	Lafontaine
ROBERT	Lafontaine
PEPIN	Laforce
LEFORT	Laforest
GARNIER	Laforge
CHAUVIN	Lafortune
PICARD	Lafortune
PILON	Lafortune
CARREAU	Lafraichèur
CHAPEAU	Laframboise
DOYON	Laframboise
GILBERT	Laframboise
DARAGON	Lafrance
BEAULNE	Lafranchise

Appendix D – *dit* Names

Surname	*dit* Name
GUERIN	Lafontaine
GUERTIN	Lesabotier
GUILBAULT	Grandbois
GUILLET	Cinqmars/St. Marc
GUILLET	Lajeunesse
GUITAUT	Jolicoeur
GUYON	Dubuisson
GUYON	Durouvray
HÉBERT	Larose
HENAULT	Canada
HOUSSARD	Le Petit
HUBOUX	Delonchamp/Delongchamps
HUNAULT/HENAULT	Deschamps
JAMME	Carrière
JANOT	Lachapelle
JARED	Beauregard
JAUFFRAY	Jolicoeur
JUILLET	d'Avignon
LACROIX	Roberge
LALANDE	Latreille
LALANDE	Mauger
LALONDE	Lesperance
LALU	Lamontagne
LAMOUREUX	St. Germain
LANGEVIN	Lacroix
LAPORTE	St. George
LAPRÉ	Petit
LAROCQUE	Rocbrune
LARUE	Deplaine
LAURARÉE	L'Orange
LAURENT	Champagne
LAVIGNE	Brisetout
LEFEBVRE	Fevre
LEFEBVRE	Laciseray
LEFORT	Laforest
LEFORT	Prairie
LEGARDEUR	Darpentigny
LEGROS	Laviolette
LEROUGE	St. Denis
LEROUX	Cardinal
LESCARBEAU	Bosseron
LESIEGE	Fontaine
LESIEUR	Calot
LOPS	Aubert
LORET	Lafontaine
LUCAS	St. Renaud
LUCOS/LUCAULT	Barbot
MAGNAN	Minier
MAHEU	Deshasards
MAILLOT	Laviolette
MAILLOUX	Desruisseau
BOURGNEUF	Lafreniere
GOYAU	Lagarde
MERCADIER	Lahaie
DEBORD	Lajeunesse
ESTEVE	Lajeunesse
GUILLET	Lajeunesse
MIGNERON	Lajeunesse
SICOTTE	Laliberté
PERTHUIS	Lalime
BADEL	Lamarche
BARITEAU	Lamarche
ST. ANDRÉ	Lamarre
DENAULT	Lamartinière
ROBILLARD	Lambert
LALU	Lamontagne
CAUCHON	Lamothe
VIÉ/VIVIER	Lamothe
DUMESNIL	Lamusique
GAUTHIER	Landreville
MARTIN	Langevin
DARVEAU	Langoumois
WATIER	Lanois/Lanoix
BANLIER	Laperle
CARPENETIER	Lapierre
MARSAN	Lapierre
MEUNIER	Lapierre
TOUPIN	Lapierre
MESSAGUÉ	Laplaine
BADAILLAC/BADAYAC	Laplante
BONNIER	Laplante
RINGUETTE	Laplante
SAUVÉ	Laplante
TESSIER	Laplante
ROBIN	Lapointe
FISSIAU	Laramée
CAMBIN	Larivière
CLEMENT	Larivière
NOLET	Larivière
ROUILLARD	Larivière
BRISSON	Laroche
BLANCHON	Larose
BOUTIN	Larose
ERODEAU	Larose
HÉBERT	Larose
MARANDA	Latourelle
DECHAUX	Latourneuse
LALANDE	Latreille
BOUCHARD	Lavallée
DUCHENY	Lavallée
FRANCOEUR	Lavallée
GIASSON	Lavallée…

Surname	*dit* Name	Surname	*dit* Name
MAISONSEULE	Majeau	PAQUET	Lavallée
MAJEAU	Maisonseule	ST. JEAN	Lavallée
MALBOEUF	Beausoleil	VALLÉE	Lavallée
MALLET	Malichon	RIQUET	Laverdure
MARANDA	Latourelle	VALIQUET	Laverdure
MARANDA	Olivier	BRODEUR	Lavigne
MAROTTE	Labonté	TESSIER	Lavigne
MARSAN	Lapierre	LEGROS	Laviolette
MARSOLET	St. Agnan	MAILLOT	Laviolette
MARTIN	L'Écossais	RANGER	Laviolette
MARTIN	Langevin	RUFIANGE	Laviolette
MARTIN	Richard	BEAUCHAMP	Le Grand Beauchamp
MARTIN	St. Jean	HOUSSARD	Le Petit
MATHON	Labrie	TABEAU	Le Petit Leveillé
MAUGER	Magny	MIVILLE	Le Suisse
MENARD	Fontaine/Lafontaine	DAMOURS	Lefret
MERCADIER	Lahaie	AVERTY	Leger
MESSAGUÉ	Laplaine	BONNEAU	Lemaitre
MESSIER	St. Francois	ROY	Lemarans
MESSIER	St. Michel	GUERTIN	Lesabotier
MEUNIER	Lapierre	LALONDE	Lesperance
MIGNAULT	Chatillon	VIAU	Lesperance
MIGNERON	Lajeunesse	BRUNET	Létang
MILLOY	Dumaine	COGNAC	Léveillé
MIVILLE	Le Suisse	CUILLERIER	Léveillé
MOISON	Parisien	NANTEAU	Linteau
MOITIÉ	Lafonderie	BENOIT	Livernois/Nivernais
MONCIAU	Desormeaux	RENAUD	Locas
MONTREUIL	Francoeur	SIMARD	Lombrette
MORIER	Veron	MAUGER	Magny
NANTEAU	Linteau	SAUVAGEAU	Maisonneuve
NOLET	Larivière	MAJEAU	Maisonseule
NOUVION	Sanscartier	MAISONSEULE	Majeau
OTIS	Fortier	MALLET	Malichon
OUCHISTAOUICHKOUE	Olivier	RICHARD	Martin
PAQUET	Bernardon	LALANDE	Mauger
PAQUET	Lavallée	MAGNAN	Minier
PAYET	St. Amour	BONIN	Morin
PELLETIER	Antaya	GRENIER	Nadeau
PEPIN	Descardonnets	MARANDA	Olivier
PEPIN	Lachance	OUCHISTAOUICHKOUE	Olivier
PEPIN	Laforce	DUPUIS	Parisien
PEPIN	Tranchemontagne	MOISON	Parisien
PERRAS	Lafontaine	LAPRÉ	Petit
PERRIER	Lafleur	BEAUDOIN	Petit Jean
PERTHUIS	Lalime	RICHAUME	Petrus
PETIT	Beauchemin	BOURGEOIS	Picard
PICARD	Lafortune	DESOISMAISONS	Picard
PILON	Lafortune	GARMAN	Picard/Le Picard
PINEAU	Deschatele	DASSILVA	Portugais
PINSONNAULT	Lafleur	PRÉ	Pothier/Poirier

Appendix D – *DIT* Names

Surname	*DIT* Name
POIRIER	Deloge/Desloge
POIRIER	Lafleur
PRÉ	Pothier/Poirier
PRESSEAU	Chambly
RAGUIDEAU	St. Germain
RANGER	Laviolette
RENAUD	Locas
RENOUARD	St. Etienne
RICHARD	Martin
RICHAUME	Petrus
RICHER	Laflêche
RINGUETTE	Laplante
RINGUETTE	Tessier
RIQUET	Laverdure
ROBERGE	Lacroix
ROBERT	Lafontaine
ROBILLARD	Lambert
ROBIN	Lapointe
ROBINEAU	Dumoulin
ROUILLARD	Larivière
ROY	Lemarans
RUFIANGE	Laviolette
SAUVAGEAU	Maisonneuve
SAUVÉ	Laplante
SEGUIN	Laderoute
SICOTTE	Laliberté
SIMARD	Lombrette
SIRET	Lafleur
SOLQUIN	St. Joseph
ST. ANDRÉ	Lamarre
ST. GODARD	Duboct
ST. JEAN	Lavallée
SURPRENANT	Sansoucy
TABEAU	Le Petit Leveillé
TESSIER	Laplante
TESSIER	Lavigne
TETU	Beauregard
TOUPIN	Lapierre
TUNÉ	Dufresne
VALIQUET	Laverdure
VALLÉE	Lavallée
VALLIÈRE	Chevalier
VEGIARD	Labonté
VERONNEAU	Denis
VIAU	Lesperance
VIÉ/VIVIER	Lamothe
WATIER	Lanois/Lanoix

Surname	*DIT* Name
BARBEAU	Potvin
BERIAU	Potvin
DESEVE	Potvin
LEFORT	Prairie
CARBONNEAU	Provençal
BEAUMONT	Rat
DUMAS	Rencontre
MARTIN	Richard
LACROIX	Roberge
DROUSSON	Robert
LAROCQUE	Rocbrune
GAUTHIER	Saguingorra
NOUVION	Sanscartier
DUHAMEL	Sansfaçon
GIRARDIN	Sansoucy
SURPRENANT	Sansoucy
GILBERT	Sanspeur
BELANGER	Simoneau
MARSOLET	St. Agnan
PAYET	St. Amour
FOUCHER	St. Aubin
DESHAIES	St. Cyr
LEROUGE	St. Denis
RENOUARD	St. Etienne
MESSIER	St. Francois
BEAUVAIS	St. Gemme
LAPORTE	St. George
LAMOUREUX	St. Germain
RAGUIDEAU	St. Germain
COITOU	St. Jean
MARTIN	St. Jean
SOLQUIN	St. Joseph
BONIN	St. Martin
BOUTET	St. Martin
DESFORGES	St. Maurice
MESSIER	St. Michel
LUCAS	St. Renaud
RINGUETTE	Tessier
BAZINET	Tourblanche
CORBEIL	Tranchemontagne
PEPIN	Tranchemontagne
GEORGET	Tranquille
MORIER	Veron
BRIEN	Villebrillan
AMIOT/AMYOT	Villeneuve
BOUCHER	Vindespagne
DESJARDINS	Zacharie

Bibliography

ancestry.ca — Internet (family trees and digitized documents)

archiv-histo — Internet (archiv-histo.com/pionniers.php)

BANQ — Bibliotheque et Archives de Québec — Internet (www.banq.qc.ca/recherche)

Bédard, Marc-André. "La Presence Protestante en Nouvelle-France", *Revue d'Histoire de l'Amerique Francaise*, v.31, no.3, 1977.

Belting, Natalia Maree. *Kaskaskia Under the French Regime.* Urbana, IL, 1948.

biographi.ca — Internet (Dictionary of Canadian Biography online)

Burton, Clarence M. *Cadillac's Village.* Detroit, 1896.

Burton, Clarence M. *Compendium of History and Biography of the City of Detroit and Wayne County, Michigan.* Detroit, 1909.

Creecy, John. *The Bodman Family in America.* Detroit, 1969.

Couillard-Despres, Azarie. *Histoire de la Seigneurie de St-Ours.* Montreal, 1915.

Dechêne, Louise. *Habitants and Merchants in Seventeenth Century Montreal.* Montreal, 1992.

Dechêne, Louise. *People, State and War Under the French Regime in Canada.* Montreal, 2021.

Dickinson, John. A. "La guerre iroquoise et la mortalité en Nouvelle-France, 1608-1666", *Revue d'histoire de l'Amérique française*, v.36, no.1, June, 1892.

Dunnigan, Brian L. *Frontier Metropolis: Picturing Early Detroit, 1701-1838.* Detroit, 2001.

Eccles, W.J. *Canada Under Louis XIV 1663-1701.* Toronto, 1964.

Eccles, W.J. "The Social, Economic and Political Significance of the Military Establishment in New France", *Canadian Historical Review*, v.52, no.1. Toronto, 1971.

fichierorigine.com — Internet (www.fichierorigine.com/recherche?numero=243774)

Fournier, Marcel. *De la Nouvelle-Angleterre à la Nouvelle-France: L'histoire des captifs anglo-américains au Canada entre 1675 et 1760.* Montreal, 1992.

Godbout, P. Archange. *Les Passager du "Saint-André".* Montreal, 1964

Gagné, Peter J. *Before the King's Daughters: The Filles à Marier 1634-1662.* Florida, 2002.

Gagné, Peter J. "Cy Devant Soldat... Apres Habitant: The Settling of the Carignan-Salières Regiment in New France". Masters thesis, Université Laval, Quebec, 2005.

Gareau, Georges R. *Boucherville: Premières Concessions d'Habitations, 1673.* Montreal, 1973.

genelogiequebec.com — Internet

Hamilton, James C. *The Panis: An Historical Outline of Canadian Indian Slavery in the 18th Century.* Toronto, 1897

Hamlin, Marie C.W. *Legends of Le Detroit.* Detroit, 1884.

Kellog, Louise Phelps. *The French Régime in Wisconsin and the Northwest.* Madison, WI, 1925.

Lajeunesse, Ernest J. *The Windsor Border Region: Canada's Southernmost Frontier.* Toronto, 1960

Landry, Yves. *Orpehelines en France, Pionnières au Canada: Les Filles du Roi au XVIIe Siècle*, 2nd ed. Quebec, 2013.

Langlois, Michel & Fournier, Marcel. *Le Régiment de Carignan-Salières: Les premieres troupes franchises de la Nouvelle-France* 1665-1668. Montreal, 2014.

Mathieu, Jacques & Kedl, Eugen. *The Plains of Abraham: The Search for the Ideal.* Ottawa, 1993.

PRDH — Internet. prdh-igd.com (Programme de Recherche en Demogaphie Historique)
   For a complete list of sources used on this site, refer to www.prdh-igd.com/en/bibliographie

St. Pierre, Telesphore. *Histoire des Canadiens de Michigan et du Comté d'Essex Ontario.* Montreal, 1895.

Seguin, André. *Seguin Dictionnaire Généalogique, 1672-2005*, 2nd ed. Boucherville, Que., 2005.

Seguin, Robert-Lionel. "Les Descendants do Francois Seguin", *Memoires de la Société Généalogique Canadienne-Française*, v.II, no.4. Montreal, 1947

Tanguay, Cyprien. *A Travers le Régistres.* Montreal, 1886.

Tanguay, Cyprien. *Dictionnaire Généalogique des Familles Canadiennes.* Montreal 1886.

Trudel, Marcel. *Canada's Forgotten Slaves: Two Hundred Years of Bondage.* Montreal, 2009.

Wilhelmy, Jean-Pierre. *Les Mercenaires Allemands au Quebec du XVIIIe Siecle et Leur Apport a la Population.* Beloeil, Que., 1984.

Index of Family Names

Numbers refer to the Lineage Charts available at www.ontariohistory.ca/seguin.pdf .

See also the General Index and *DIT* Names in Appendix D.

Achon 132
Aguenier 114
Alain 119
Alère 404
Allen 106, 115, 419
Amiot/Amyot 86, 162, 408.1
Archambault 79.1, 116, 124, 130, 131, 136, 143, 161, 278, 433, 466, 483
Ardion 517
Ardouin 83
Arnaud 177
Arnault 471.2
Arnoux 116
Arnus 185, 511
Aselly 159
Asselin 149
Aubé 168
Aubert 427
Aubourg 182
Audet 414
Audiau 134, 145
Auger 96, 147
Auneau 108, 425, 459
Auvray 168
Avrard 484
Ayotte 168, 492

Babin 73
Badaillac 180, 506
Badel 173, 495
Bagaton 426
Bahmahmaadjimiw 444
Banlier 165
Banne 73, 159, 402, 481

Baratin 421
Barbant 106, 427
Barbary 126, 450
Barbe 11, 84, 107
Barbeau 10, 18, 73
Barbier 416, 484
Bard 162
Baret 131
Baril 157, 174
Bariteau 146
Barré 125, 447
Barreau 12, 90
Barsa 128, 452
Basmont 170
Basset 485
Baudon 186, 512
Bazinet 182
Beauchamp 108, 110, 424
Beaudoin 161, 167, 513
Beaudry 175
Beaulne 82
Beaumont 154, 474
Beauvais 75, 111, 113
Belanger 24, 81, 179, 503
Bellemanière 431
Belleville 440
Bellier 511
Bénard 182, 502
Benoit 145, 423, 469
Berger 515
Bernard 95, 140, 462.3
Berteau 159, 481
Bertesol 170
Bertin 85
Bertrand 119

Betfer/Bedford 142, 441, 465
Bias 159
Bideau 145
Bigot 438
Billard 76
Bilodeau 111, 430
Bineau 486
Biré 118, 435
Biroleau 10, 78
Bissonnet 21, 153
Bizelan 78
Blain 516
Blanchard 122, 126, 428, 448
Blois 450
Blondeau 79.1, 491
Boigeou 178
Boire 402
Boiscochin 122
Boisdon 122
Boismé 118, 436
Boivin 79.1
Bonin 25, 184, 461
Bonne 465
Bonneau 516
Bonnet 436
Bonnier 96
Borel 166
Bouchard 16, 19, 122, 132, 142
Boucher 3, 24, 100, 123, 149, 174, 177, 232, 443, 487, 489
Bouet 432
Boulanger 431
Boulard 124
Boulet 19, 141

Bourassa   123, 445
Bourdon   77
Bourgeois   497
Bourgery   82, 137, 406, 461
Bousquet   22, 165
Boutet   171, 493
Bouthillier   21, 155
Boutin   11, 80, 144
Boutine   113
Boyer   12, 14, 18, 92, 93, 101, 136, 409
Brassard   80, 166, 180, 489, 507
Brazeau   10, 76
Breault   3, 22, 158, 439
Breché   504
Bregouin   511
Brelancour   174
Bretel   161
Bretonnet   421
Breuse   21
Briault/Barreau   13, 99
Brière   423, 486, 505
Brisset   97
Brodeur   153, 511
Brossard   19, 134, 145
Brosseau   116
Broue   418
Broust   426
Brunet   10, 15, 17, 75, 87, 100, 110, 111, 113, 126, 428, 448
Buisson   120, 440
Bunel   102

Cadieux   10, 77
Caillé   83, 103
Cailleteau   480
Caillonneau   170
Campagna   187, 517
Campeau   18, 134
Camus   157, 170, 173, 479, 494
Canin   480
Cantau   88

Carbonneau   125
Cardillon   84, 128
Caron   103, 133, 143, 458
Carreau   178, 502
Carroll   123
Catin   134
Cauchon   458
Caussade   502
Cavelier   167
Ceillier   490, 90
Chagneau   79.2
Chalifoux   116, 433
Chamard   118, 437
Chancy   127, 451
Chanloy   81
Chapacou   155, 187, 476, 515
Chapeau   189
Chapelain   121, 154, 442, 469, 473
Chapman   419
Charbonneau   16, 120, 124, 131, 439, 446
Charles   130, 455, 460, 479
Charlot   174, 415
Charpentier   516
Charron   169
Chartrand   16, 121
Chassé   517
Chauvet   514
Chauvin   161, 179, 483, 518, 73, 402
Chefdeville   130, 454
Chené/Chenet   424
Chenu   424
Chevalier   94, 101, 491
Chichon   408.1
Choseau   452
Choublet   155
Clavier   510
Clement   17, 127
Cloques   183
Cloutier   163, 179, 486, 505, 513
Cognac   20, 144, 467

Cogu   463
Coiffé   151, 403
Coignet   132
Cointel   458
Coitou   79.1
Collet   153
Confland   79.2, 188
Content   117, 434
Cordeau   79.1
Cordelette   134
Cormier   468
Corneau   109
Coron   17, 131
Coshet   455
Cotin   186
Cotin   512
Couillard   111, 163, 430, 485
Coulonne   481
Courtin   462.2
Cousin   147, 470
Cousseau   77
Cousteau   214, 422
Couvent   86, 408.1, 413
Crepin   436
Creusette   81
Crevet   458
Crissot   94
Cronier   75
Cuillerier   15, 109
Curé   137, 460
Curier   407
Curtis   419
Cusson   3, 20, 23, 90, 146, 171
Cyr   131

Daigneau   12, 88
Dailleboust   151
Damisé   135
Damour   150, 471.2
Damy   98, 417
Dania   155, 477
Daoust   15, 110, 427
Daragon   156
Dardenne   108, 424

Darmine 497
Darveau 117
Daunais 185
Dauphin 24, 178, 500
David 75, 111, 422, 429
Davignon 435
Debenne 94
Debournelle 139
Decelles 101, 156, 418, 478
Dechaux 121, 154, 442, 473
Delage 172
Delaney 139, 416, 444
Delaplace 158
Deliercourt 183, 510
Delières 21, 156
Delomé 166, 490
Delpeche 159, 482
Demers 92
Demers/Dumais 130, 411, 454
Demeslier 72
Demontaguerre 165
Denevers 168, 492
Denois 411
Denommé/Delomé 24, 180
Denoyon 73, 111, 429
Depiennes 509
Deplaine 484
Deroulette 129
Dervie 449
Dery 119
Desacepée 76, 125
Desavis 447
Descene 91
Deschamps 11
Desforges 95
Desjardins 17, 84, 128
Desnoyers 79.3
Desportes 141, 463, 491
Despres 164, 506
Destroismaisons 138
Devarennes 143
Deveau 184, 188
Devincennes 78

Devoisy 174
Dionet 104
Dobigeon 98
Dodin 88, 408.2
Doigt 119
Doucinet 88, 121
Doyon 157
Drouet 118, 437
Drouin 179, 505
Drusson 150
Dubeau 98, 417, 447
Dubois 84, 128, 432, 505
Ducharme 93
Duchêne 149, 162, 175, 496
Ducheny 149
Duchesne 173, 495
Dufort 15, 112
Dugas 435
Dumas 89
Dumesnil 20, 149, 478, 516
Dupen 472
Duplan 152
Dupont 486, 505
Duprac 177
Dupré 105
Dupuis 98, 173
Duquette 2, 12, 86
Durand 133
Durandel 430
Duron 82
Dussault 123, 183, 444
Dutrain 201
Duval 103, 106, 176

Emard 163, 486
Emery 184, 188
Énard 119, 438
Esnault 468
Ethier 124
Eysley 419

Fafard 519
Faille 93
Faitfeu 109

Feillard 518
Fevrier 23, 151, 173
Fissiau 23, 172
Folure 184
Fontaine 80
Forestier 77, 403
Forget 152, 153
Fortier 151
Foubert 90, 146, 171
Fouchard 445
Fouquet 152
Foureau 77
Fourier 165, 122, 141, 153, 517
Franchort 73, 429
Francoeur 91, 149
Francois 467
Fremillon 519
Froment 23, 167

Gaboury 186, 433, 513
Gabriel 84, 128
Gadoury 186, 25
Gageut 141
Gagné 13, 19, 98, 132, 139, 416
Gagnon 133, 458
Gaillard 126, 449
Galarde 507
Gallien 14, 103, 176
Gandin 144, 467
Gareau 157, 480
Garman 97, 117, 174, 415
Garnier 120, 124, 131, 439, 446, 470, 499
Gasse 406
Gateau 516
Gaudet 88
Gaudreau 72
Gaudry 168, 491
Gauthier 86, 100, 168, 171, 173, 407, 494, 508
Gauvin 409

Gavatte   185
Gendron   187, 516
Genet   474
Genus   14, 102
Georget   13, 97
Geraume   417
Gesseaume   454
Giasson   140
Gibeau   158
Gilbert   24, 181
Gilles   134
Gillis   121
Girard   2, 11, 79.2, 79.3, 140
Girardin   113, 431
Girault   109
Giroux   24, 176, 498
Gladu   24, 175
Gobinet   145, 469
Godard   156, 176, 498
Godefroy   471.1
Godin   81, 149, 232
Gordien   93
Gosselin   109
Gosset   105
Gouion   107
Goulet   25
Goulet   188, 518
Goupillots   153
Goyeau   155
Granger   160
Graton   177
Greete   419
Grenier   120, 141, 441
Grignon   180
Grondin   158, 182
Gronier   434, 138
Grossin   415
Guertin   157, 170, 479
Guibour   185
Guichaut   488
Guignard   178, 501
Guigne   512
Guilbault   25, 187, 514

Guillebonne   170
Guillemette   156, 478
Guillet   76, 107, 163, 214, 422
Guilminet   414
Guitaut   92, 412
Gurry   139, 154, 472
Guyon   22, 140, 162, 163, 179, 462.3, 471.1, 484, 485, 503

Hamel   23, 168
Hamelin   496
Harbory   97
Hardy   74, 135
Harouard   483
Hébert   141, 463, 485, 145
Hedin   127
Henault   2, 14, 105
Heritier   150
Hodiau   468
Hubert   85
Huboux   120, 142, 441, 465
Huet   484
Hugo   149
Hulon   455
Humphrey   1
Hunault   15, 108, 110, 423
Hurteau   172
Hus   118, 126, 436

Icarde   128

Jacques   181
Jamme   126
Janot   182, 509
Jarnet   88, 408.2
Jetté   130, 455
Joanne   188
Joannet   457
Jolivet   113, 431
Joly   502
Josnau   184
Jourdain   159, 183, 482
Kienten   13
Kimball   106, 419

L'Archeveque   79.3, 404
L'Homme   145, 408.2
Labelle   2, 17, 124
Labourier   117
Labraye   415
Lacoste   188
Lacroix   3, 23
Lafond   163, 487
Lagoutte   181
Lagueux   122
Lahaie   183
Lainé   117, 434
Lalande   11, 82
Lalonde   14, 15, 106, 110, 115, 427
Lamarche   150, 175, 497
Lamberton   106, 420
Lamothe   129
Lamoureux   101, 177
Landelle   471.1
Landry   72, 125, 447
Langevin   164
Langlois   175, 177, 451, 456, 463, 491, 499
Laper   91
Laporte   175, 496
Larivière   82, 90
Larose   136
Latier   129, 453
Launière   410
Laurence   22, 159
Laurent   160
Lauzon   10, 79.1, 124, 131, 278
Laval   495
Laveau   183
Lavergne   511
Lavigne   21, 152
Lavoie   81, 85, 189
Lawlor   180, 506
Le Noir   278, 466
Lebas   428, 448
Leblanc   508
Leboeuf   154, 475
Lebrun   126, 450

Index of Family Names

Leclerc 123, 166, 180, 443, 490
Lecompte 411
Lecornu 475
Lecours 94
Ledoux 22, 164
Ledran 94, 413
Leduc 479
Lefebvre 135, 108, 110, 187, 425, 459, 493, 514
Lefort 20, 150
Lefrancois 160166, 488
Legendre 82, 406, 461
Leger 89, 91, 443
Legrand 151, 173, 434
Legris 77
Lehoux 133, 457
Lejeune 182
Lelievre 93
Lelong 89
Lemaire 105, 487
Lemaitre 92, 171, 410
Lemelin 166, 489
Lemieux 154, 475
Lemoine 153, 162, 404, 440
Lenoblet 106
Lepelle 471.1
Lepere 91
Lepine 160
Lepotier 75
Lerouge 178, 502
Leroux 105, 138, 519, 181, 508
Lescalier 141
Lescarbeau 22, 161, 167
Leseur 91
Lesiege 158
Letourneau 21, 154, 472
Levaigneur 480
Levasseur 459
Levert 129, 453
Lewen 420
Liret 165
Loiseau 137, 201, 460, 487

Long 1
Longral 408.1, 413
Lopez 164
Lops 85
Loret 76, 125
Lorgeleux 469
Lorgueil 108, 423
Loué 124
Loyer 501
Loysel 456
Lucier 175, 497
Lucos/Lucault 109, 426
Lumoi 170
Luosbisce 492

MacDonell 1
Maclin 136
Magnan/Minier 16, 119
Maheu 179
Maigne 515
Maillot 187, 515
Mailloux 1
Maisonneuve 17, 129
Majeau 25, 183
Major 445
Malboeuf 3, 19, 138
Malle 83
Mallet 10, 12, 74, 87, 131, 135, 232, 443
Manchon 107, 421
Maranda 147, 470
Marchand 79.3
Margane 79.3
Maricour 227
Marier 76, 125, 129
Marmauts 495
Marotte 19, 144
Marsan 78
Marsolet 162, 484
Martaguet 165
Martel 147
Martin 14, 104, 130, 136, 133, 140, 151, 169, 449, 456, 462.2, 516, 517

Massé 107, 422
Massieu 72
Masson 103, 176, 185
Mathieu 227
Mathon 88, 121
Maudeme 98
Mauger 86, 134, 454
Maupas 141
Mechin 137
Meilleur 457
Melaine 489
Meliot 81
Mémé 143
Menacier 94, 413
Menard 20, 77, 142, 151, 403, 422, 512
Mercier 458
Méry 80, 405, 489, 507
Messagué 11, 83, 127
Messier 22, 162, 153
Metro 189
Metru 94
Meunier 25, 185, 189, 470, 519
Meurfois/Murphy 84
Michel 132, 139, 450
Migeau 108, 201
Mignault 155, 186, 513
Migneron 96, 159, 414
Millau 475
Millet 172, 499
Miloy 147, 471.1
Mineau 103
Miville 86, 162
Moison 137, 462.1
Moitie 20, 148
Mondy 494
Monet 172
Monier 98, 145, 468
Montigny 488
Montreuil 157, 480
Morais 89
Moreau 93, 491
Morel 429

115

Morier 103
Morin 19, 22, 92, 140, 160, 168,
 178, 411, 432, 491, 500
Morisseau 23, 170, 174
Motel 514
Mouillard 121
Moulin 465
Moulinet 169
Moutier 88
Mulier 188
Mulier 518
Murphy/Meurfois 84

Nicolet 123, 444
Nieding 13
Nigremont 490
Ninet 112
Nion 80
Noel 186
Noget 74
Noire 483
Nolet 20, 147, 496
Nommaire 103, 176
Nouvion 3, 21
Nyeullé 232

Olivier/Wendat 176, 217, 425, 459
Omelet 116
Ouellette 1
Ouvrard 278, 466, 483

Pacaud 155, 184, 476, 515
Pageot 16, 118
Pain 442, 473
Painter 106, 420
Pajot 463
Pannier 462.3

Paquet/Pasquier 2, 16, 116, 154, 189, 474, 519
Paradis 147, 471.1
Paré 133, 183, 457

Parmentier 443
Patin 510
Paulo 134
Pavie 96, 414
Payant 109
Payet 17, 130, 136
Pedigars 402
Peinbaut 144
Peineau 136
Pelletier 174
Pellissonneau 511
Pennetier 165
Pepin 18, 90, 137, 139
Peroche 140
Perras 92, 410
Perreault 20
Perrier 126, 449
Perthuis 18, 135
Pesard 97
Pescot 515
Petit 72, 79.1, 125, 172, 424
Philippeau 119, 171, 438, 493
Picard 14, 107, 120, 183, 413, 510
Pichon 86, 407, 494
Pilon 110, 428
Piloy 128, 452
Pilusasdier 161
Pinard 480, 506
Pineau 491
Pinson 160
Pinsonnault 91
Pinsonneau 467
Pioche 135
Pipette 437
Piton/Pisson 128
Place 148
Planteson 79.2
Plat 169
Plouart 152
Poete 179, 504
Poirier 2, 14, 100, 462.2
Poisson 100, 101, 109, 418, 426
Poitras 11, 85
Poupart 430
Poussard 116
Poussin 79.3
Presseau 127, 451
Prévert 13, 95
Prieur 487
Proulx 78
Provencher 107, 421
Provost/Prévost 164, 176, 217
Ptolomée 137, 462.1

Quenneville 17, 76, 125
Queval 121
Quilleron 498

Rabeau 499
Rabouin 187, 517
Racicot 135
Racine 133, 456
Rainville 179, 504
Ramage 81
Rancin 79.2, 188
Ranger 15, 113
Ratelle 105
Ravenelle 101
Recheine 428, 448
Regnard 76
Renaud 80
Renaud 132, 181, 508
Renouard 83, 127
Renoule 78
Retonel 409
Ribeau 96
Riberon 143
Ribou 92, 412
Richard 185, 500
Richaume 185, 511
Richer 95, 227, 507, 180
Ricouet 412
Ringuette 178

Index of Family Names

Rival 89
Riverin 509
Roberge 166
Robert 137, 461
Robillard 3, 25, 182
Robin 471.1, 485, 503, 484
Rocheteau 80
Rochon/Rocheron 120, 440
Roger 458
Roissier 79.2
Rolet 463, 485
Rolland 500
Roquet 418
Rosée 98, 416
Rotrau 138
Rouault 118, 428
Rouette 460
Rouillard 79.3
Roule 424
Rousseau 116
Roussel 100, 412
Routhier 11, 25, 81, 189
Roy 12, 93, 113, 118, 432, 435, 471.1
Rozier 462.1
Ruel 147
Ruelland 74
Rufiange 12, 89
Rutan 493

Sade 117
Sage 420
Samson 2, 13, 94
Saute 478
Sauvage 83
Sauvageau 464, 142
Savinelle 151, 403
Scott 419
Sederay 107, 120
Seguin 1, 2, 3, 10, 18, 72, 173

Sénécal 12, 91, 99
Serre 156
Simard 18, 133
Simon 79.3, 404
Solde 75
Soret 517
Sorin 178, 501
Soulage 493
Soyer 181
St. Jean 149
St. Père 163, 214, 422
Steele 465
Suire 517
Suliere 93

Tabeau 113, 432
Tabit 142, 464
Tallonnier 139
Tardé 150, 471.2
Taurel 175
Tellier 452
Tenard 92, 409
Tesseran 482
Tessier 19, 130, 136, 143, 178, 180
Teste 139
Therrien 138
Thiboutot 16, 123
Tibou 519
Touchard 132
Touchetelle 119
Toupin 24, 177
Toureau 79.1, 143, 278, 433, 466, 483
Travers 144
Tremblay 18, 132
Trepé 451
Triaud 166, 488
Trottain 122
Trottier 108, 110, 163, 201, 487

Trouvé 158
Trut 97, 117, 415
Tuné 135, 459

Vachon 177, 499
Vacquemoulin 407
Vadois 85
Vaillant 155, 477
Valade 77
Valin 16, 117
Valiquet 164
Vallée 123, 187, 445, 462.1, 516
Vallerand 13, 96
Vallière 122
Vandoren 438
Vara 146
Vegiard 23, 169
Verdon 95, 227
Vernin 165
Veronneau 21, 157
Viau 152
Viel 101
Vienne 101
Viens 217
Vigneau 140, 462.2
Vilenne 484
Voisin 441

Wabenaki 217
Wanne 1
Watier 15, 114
Whatlock 419

Yvon 440

General Index

Numbers refer to <u>page numbers</u> in this book.

Indigenous subjects are marked ‡

ALL CAPS are used for direct ancestors of Theodore and Alphonsine

See also the Family Name Index and *DIT* Names in Appendix D

A

Abenaki — see Wabanaki ‡

Acadia (*l'Acadie*)   20, 21, 51

Acadie (New Brunswick and Nova Scotia) — see Acadia

African slave — see Le Jeune, Olivier

Albany (Fort Orange), NY   24, 32, 44

Algonkian language ‡   41

Algonquin ‡   16, 23, 41, 44, 53
 — see also Anishinaabe

ALLEN, Sarah (Marie Madeleine HÉLÈNE)   46, 50, App. A-14

ALLEN family   50

Allier Regiment   29

Allumette Island   53

Amariton Company, *Troupes de la Marine*   57

American War of Independence (1775-1783)   39, 64, 65

Anglo-Dutch War (1665-1667)   31

Anglo-French War (1627-1629)   21

Anishinaabe ‡   15, 16, 17, 19, 23, 24, 41, 53, 57
 - see also Algonquin

Anishinaabe language ‡   17

Apache ‡   17

ARCHAMBAULT, Anne   47

Atlantic Ocean   21, 29

B

BADEL, André   50

BAHMAHMAADJIMIWIN, Gisis, called Jeanne ‡   53, 54, App. A-3

Baie d'Urfé, Que   46

Baie des Puans — see Green Bay, Wisconsin

BANNE, Marie Gillette   49

BARBE, Abel Joseph   50

BARBEAU, Genevieve   60

BARBIER, Marie   21, 22

BASMONT, Marie Anne   50

Baton Rouge, Louisiana   56

Battle of Carillon   38, 39, 39n

Battle of Chateauguay   106

Battle of Lake George   38

Battle of Montmorency   39

Battle of Oriskany   40

Battle of Ste. Foy   39

Battle of the Plains of Abraham   39

Bay of Fundy   21

Bay of Quinte   60

Béarn Regiment   38, 39, 100

BEAUSOLEIL, Julie   6, 66

Beauvais, France   9, 20

Belgium   14, 23, 50

Belle Isle — see *Ile aux Cochons*

Belle River, Ont.   59, 69

BERTEAU,
 Elisabeth Isabelle   48-49
 Jacques   49

BETFER (Bedford), Suzanne   50

BIROLEAU, Pierre   57

BOUCHER *dit* Lacroix, Henriette   67

Boucher, Pierre — seigneur   35

Boucherville, Que.   19, 35, 49, 69, 99

BOURDON, Jacques   35

BOYER *dit* Lafontaine, Marie Catherine   65

119

BREAULT *dit* Lafleur,
   Antoine   100
   Delima   68
   Méderic   67

British Army   39

Brittany, France   23

Brock, Maj. Gen. Sir Isaac   100

Burlington Bay, Ont.   61

Caddoan language ‡   17

Cadillac, Sieur Antoine Laumet de Lamotte   57

Calvinists   16, 50, 51, 52

CAMPEAU,
   Archange   63, 65
   Jean-Baptiste   64

Captives   16-19, 41-46, App. A-13, A-14, A-15

Cardinal, Francoise Cunegondé ‡   19

Carignan- Salières Regiment   20, 28-34, 35, 42, 50, 56, 98, 99

Carrying Place, Bay of Quinte, Ont.   60

Cataraqui (now Kingston, Ont.)   56, 57

Cayuga (Iroquois) ‡   24, 30, 56

Chambellé Regiment   29

Champlain, Samuel   41, 42, 51, 53

Champlain's Habitation (Quebec City)   21-23

CHAPACOU, Simon   48

Chaussegros de Léry, Gaspard   61, 62

CHAUVIN, Michel   47

Cholet *dit* Laviolette, Sébastien   45

Chomedy, Paul — see Maisonneuve

Christian religion   16-19, 45, 50, 56

Cluett, Marjorie   2, 5, 44, 45, App. A-13

Cocheco, New Hampshire (now Dover, NH).   44, 45

COGNAC *dit* Léveillé, Pierre   38

Combaud, Charles   49

Compagnie de la Nouvelle France   20

Compagnie de St. Sulpice   26

Compagnie des Cents-Associés   20, 21, 24, 51, 53

Compagnies Franches de la Marine — see *Troupes de la Marine*

Company of One Hundred Associates — see *Compagnie des Cents-Associés*

Cosmouette, Louise — see Cursinwhitt, Abigail

COUILLARD, Guillaume   47

Courcelles, Daniel Remy — governor of New France (1665-1672)   30, 31

Crown Point, NY — see Fort St. Frédéric

Cursinwhitt, Abigail (Louise Cosmouette)   44, 45

CUSSON *dit* L'Ange, George   100

CUSSON, Marcelline   66

DAIGNEAU, René   19, 49, 57, 58, App. A-17

Dakota Sioux (Isanyathi) ‡   17

DAVID, Claude   56, 56n

Deerfield, Massachusetts   44, 46, 50, App. A-14

DELIÈRES, Joseph Amable   64

Denonville, Marquis — governor of New France   42

DENOYON, Jean-Baptiste   35

Department of Marine and Colonies   36

DESFORGES, Marie Genevieve   18

DESPORTES,
   Hélène   22, App. A-8, A-9
   Pierre   22

Détroit du Lac Erié — see Detroit, Michigan

Detroit River region   58, 59, 61, 62, 64, 65, 69, 101

Detroit, Michigan   57, 59-64, 69, 71, 100, App. A-16, A-17

DEVOISY, Jeanne   47

Douglas Company, Languedoc Regiment   38

Dover, NH   44

DOYON *dit* Laframboise, Nicolas ‡   19, 54, App. A-7

DOYON, Marie Josephte   19

DUCHESNE, Barbe   50

DUFORT *dit* Lacouture, Jean-Baptiste   100

Dulhut Company, *Troupes de la Marine*   57

Dumont de Balignac, Gabriel   49

DUQUETTE *dit* Desrochers,
   Paul   100
   Philomene   69n, App. A-19

DUSSAULT, Elie   16

Dutch   24, 29, 31, 41

Edict of Nantes, 1598   50, 51
England   23, 50
English people   14, 22, 24, 31, 33, 35, 40-42, 44, 46, 47, 50
English language   71
Essex County, Ont.   13, 59, 65-69
Execution   48, 49

Filles à marier   26-27
Filles du Roi   20, 27
Finger Lakes, NY   41
Five Nations Confederacy — see Cayuga, Mohawk, Oneida, Onondaga, Seneca — see also Iroquois ‡
Flanders, Belgium   50
Fort Carillon (Fort Ticonderoga)   38
Fort Chambly   29, 33, 38
Fort Detroit   57, 62, 64, 100 — see also Fort Pontchartrain du Détroit
Fort Frontenac (Kingston, Ont.)   39, 54, 56, 57, 60
Fort Orange (Albany, NY)   24, 31
Fort Oswego   39
Fort Pontchartrain du Détroit   57, 60 — see also Fort Détroit
Fort Richelieu (Sorel, Que.)   30
Fort St. Frédéric (Crown Point, NY).   38
Fort St. Louis   29, 30
Fort Stanwix   40
Fort William Henry   38
FRANCOEUR *dit* Lavallée, Francois   17
French and Indian War — see Seven Years War
French Army   28, 29, 31, 35, 38, 39
French River, Ont.   60
Fur-trade   18, 20, 22-24, 30, 35, 36, 41, 53, 55-57, 60, 61

GABOURY, Antoine   47
GAGNÉ, Marie Angelique   40
Gaillard, Marie   17
Galisonniere, Roland-Michel Barrin — governor of New France (1651-1657)   60

Ganaraska River (Port Hope, Ont.)   56
Ganaraske village (Port Hope, Ont.) ‡   61
Gandatsetiagon village (Pickering, Ont.) ‡   61
GAREAU,
  Marie Louise   19
  Pierre   35
Garman "Gannonchiase", Charles — son of Pierre
GARMAN, Pierre   19
Gelnhaar, Germany   39
Geneva, Switzerland   50
Georgian Bay, Ont.   55, 56, 60
German   14, 23, 39, 40, 50
GILBERT *dit* Comtois, Louis   57
GIRARD, Francois   101
Gladstone Avenue, Windsor, Ont.   70
GLADU, Nicolas   44
Gloucester, England,   50
Gonnentenre, Marie (Oneida) ‡   19
Grand Marais (Great Marsh), Detroit, Michigan   62
Grand River, Ont.   61
Grande Recrue   24-25
Great Peace of Montreal (1701)   57, 60
Greely, Aaron — surveyor   63
Green Bay (*Baie des Puans*), Wisconsin   54, 56, 57
Groseilliers, Médard Chouart   56
Grosse Pointe, Ml.   62
Guillet, Pierre — ship captain   29
Gulf of Mexico   17, 20, 56

Hardy, Anne   13, App. A-2
Hatfield, Massachusetts   44
Haudecoeur, Jean   49
Haudenausonee ‡ — see Cayuga, Mohawk, Oneida, Onondaga, Seneca — see also Iroquois, Five Nations
Heard,
  Hannah (Herd, Marie Anne)   45, App. A-13
  John   45, App. A-13
HÉBERT,
  Guillaume   22
  Louis   20-22, App. A-8

Hébert, Marie Jeanne   47
HÉLÈNE, Marie Madeleine — see ALLEN, Sarah
Henry IV, King of France   50
Hesse-Hanau, Germany   39, 50
Hôtel-Dieu hospital, Quebec City   29, 48
Hudson River   41
Hudson River valley   24, 54
Huguenots   50, 51 — see also Calvinists
Hull, Elizabeth   45, App. A-13
Hull, General William   100
Humphrey, Margaret   72
HUNAULT *dit* Deschamps, Toussaint   49
Huron — see Wendat ‡   49

*I*le aux Cochons (now Belle Isle)   62
Illinois, Indigenous nation ‡   19, 57
Illinois, state   18, 41, 57, 60, 64
ILLINOISE, Anastasie — Anishinaabe Illinois woman ‡   19, 57
Indiana   64
Inter-tribal warfare ‡   41
Iroquois ‡   16, 19, 20, 24, 28, 29, 33, 35, 36, 41-44, 46, 54-57, 60, 61, 99, App. A-15
Iroquois villages ‡   54, 61

Jaeger Corps — see von Kreuzbourg's Jaeger Corps
Jasselin, Marguerite   49
Jefferson Avenue, Detroit, MI   62
Jennings,
  Captivity   44
  Stephen   44
Jesuit missionaries   55, 56
Jourdeau Company, Béarn Regiment   39

Kahnawake Reserve ‡   45
Kaskaskia (Caskoukia), Illinois   54, 57, 60
Kentio, Cayuga village ‡   56
Kimball family   50
King Philip's War (1675-1676)   44

King William's War (Nine Years War, 1688-1697)   42, 44
Kingston, Ont.   39, 56, 60
Kirke brothers   21-22, 47

La Barre — governor of New France   57
La Justice — ship   20, 29, 47, 98
La Nativité — ship   27
La Prairie, Que.   40, 49
La Présentation mission (Ogdensburg, NY)   60
La Rochelle, France   16, 20, 23, 28, 29
Lac de Deux Montagnes, Que.   69
Lachenaie, Que.,   35
Lachine Massacre   42, 43
Lachine rapids   60
Lacorne de Chaptes Company, *Troupes de la Marine*   57
Lake Champlain   33, 38, 41
Lake Erie   57, 60, 61
Lake George   33, 38
Lake Huron   56, 57
Lake Michigan (*Lac des Ilinois*)   54, 56
Lake Nipissing   15, 53, 60
Lake Ontario   16, 39, 41, 54, 60, 61
Lake St. Clair.   62
Lake Superior   56
LALONDE, Guillaume   46
Lambert family   50
LAMOUREUX *dit* St. Germain, Pierre   19
Lanaudière region, Que.   67
LANGLOIS,
  Francoise   22
  Marguerite   22
Languedoc Regiment   38, 39
LAPORTE, Marie Louise   44
Latouche, Julien   48, 49
LAURENCE, Noel   49
LAVIGNE, Marie Anne   39
LAWLOR, Catherine   50

Le Bailiff   47
Le Général – ship   57
Le Jeune, Oliver – enslaved person   47
Le Joyeux Siméon – ship – see *Le St. Siméon*
Le Saint André, ship   26
Le Saint Siméon, ship   29
LEDOUX, Louis   48
LEFORT, Marie Josephte   38
Lelièvre, Mathurin   49
LETOURNEAU, Pierre   64
Limoges, France,   37
LOISEAU, Lucas   35
London, Eng.   50
Long Point, Lake Erie, Ont.   61
Long, Nancy   72
LOPEZ, Marie Renée   48
Lorraine, France   28
Louis XIV, King of France   27, 51
Louisiana (*la Louisiane*)   20, 56, 60, 64
Lowell, Massachusetts   67
LUCOS, Léonard   24, App. A-11

Macdonell, Shirley   71
Maidstone Township   68
MAILLOT *dit* Laviolette
Mailloux,
   Camille   72
   Michelle   3, 72
   Patrick   72
   Paul   72
   Peter   72
Maine   21, 45
Maisonneuve, Paul Chomedy – founder of Montreal   24
MALLET,
   Marie Catherine   57
   Pierre   13, 57, App. A-2, A-16
Mance, Jeanne – founder of Montreal   24
MANITOUABEOUICH, Roch (Wendat) ‡   16
Marsal, France   28

MARSOLET *dit* St. Agnan, Nicolas   21-22, 47
MARTIN *dit* L'Écossais, Abraham   22, 39, App. A-10
Massachusetts state   44, 46, 50, 67
MASSIEU., Marie   20
MATHON, Madeleine   49
Mattawa River, Ont.   60
MAUGER, Charlotte   50
McNiff, Patrick – surveyor   62, 63
MENARD *dit* Lafontaine, Jacques   35
MESSIER *dit* St. Michel, Michel   56-57, App. A-15
Michigan   13, 57, 63, 64
MIGNAULT, Jeanne   47
Migrants   17-40, 47, 50, 51, 57-59, 60, 64, 69
Missions   16, 36, 45, 46, 55-57, 60
Mississippi River   20, 56, 57
Missouri - state   57
MIVILLE *dit* Le Suisse, Pierre   47, 50
Mohawk (Iroquois) ‡   24, 30, 31, 33, 41, 42, 45, 56
Montagnais ‡   19, 21, 23, 24, 41
Montcalm Ave., Windsor, Ont.   70
Montcalm, General Louis-Joseph   38, 39
Montreal, Que.   16-19, 23-26, 28, 33, 39, 40, 45, 48-50, 56, 57, 60, 61, 99, 100, App. A-11
MORIN, Noel   22, App. A-9
MORISSEAU, Louis   101

Nebraska   17, 19
New Amsterdam – see New York City
New Brunswick (l'Acadie)   20, 21, 65
New England   44-46
New France (*la Nouvelle France*) – definition   20
New Hampshire   44
New York City (New Amsterdam)   24
New York, state   31, 41
Newfoundland (*la Terre Neuve*)   20
Niagara River   57
NICOLET,
   Jean   15, 53-56
   Marie Madeleine Euphrosine   15-16, 53
NIEDING, Gebhardt   39-40, 50, App. A-12

Nine Years War (King William's War, 1688-1697) 42, 44

Nipissing (Anishinaabe) (*Nepisnguée*) ‡ 15, 38, 53, 54

Normandy, France 23

Notre Dame Catholic church, Quebec City 16

NOUVION,
Jacques 38, 39
Joseph 100

Nova Scotia (*l'Acadie*) 20, 21, 65

Ogdensburg, NY 60

Ojibway (Anishinaabe) ‡ 23

Oléron Island, France 29

OLIVIER, Marie (Marie SYLVESTRE) ‡ 16, App. A-4

Oneida (Iroquois) ‡ 19, 24, 30

Onondaga (Iroquois) (*Onontague*) ‡ 16, 24, 30, 41

Orléans Regiment 29

Oswego, NY 60

Ottawa River 53, 63, 69

Ouchibahanoukoueou ‡ 16

Ouchistauichkoue, Marie OLIVIER (Marie SYLVESTRE) — see OLIVIER, Marie ‡

Ouellette, Loretta 2, 45, 72, App. A-18

PACAUD, Marie-Vincente 48

Painter family 50

Panis ‡ — see Pawnee — see also Slaves

Papineauville, Que. 69

Paris, France 16, 23, 26, 27

Parke Davis & Co., Detroit 69, 70, 71

Pawnee (Panis) ‡ 17, 19, 54

Pays d'en Haut — see Upper Country

PELLETIER *dit* Antaya, Francois 19

Perche, France 23

Perkins, Que. 69

PERTHUIS, Pierre 56, 57

PETIT, Jeanne, fille du Roi and wife of Francois SEGUIN *dit* Laderoute 20, 27, 35 — see also SEGUIN *dit* Laderoute for her descendants

Picardie, France. 20, 37

Picarouiche, Marie Francoise (Anishinaabe) ‡ 19

Pierre Street, Tecumseh, Ont. 70

Pike Creek, Ont. 66

Plains of Abraham, Quebec City 39, App. A-10 — see also MARTIN *dit* L'Écossais, Abraham

Platte River region, Nebraska 17, 19

Poignet, Francois 49

Point Pelee 61

Pointe Coupée, Louisiana 56, 60

POIRIER *dit* Desloge, Michel 101

POIRIER,
Exilda 69
Joseph, 57

Poitou Regiment 29

Pontiac's War, 1763 46

Port Royal, Nova Scotia 20, 21

Potawatomi (Anishinaabe) ‡ 17

Praying Indians ‡ 45

PRÉVERT (or PRÉVOST), Jean-Baptiste ‡ 17-19, 54, App. A-6

PRÉVOST,
Marie Therese 16
Martin 16

Prince Edward County, Ont. 56, 61

Protestants — see Calvinists — see also Puritans

Prudhomme, Pierre 45

Puritans 44, 46, 50

Quebec City, Que. 16, 19, 21-24, 26, 28, 29, 33, 35, 38, 39-41, 47, 48, 53, 56

Queen Anne's War, 1702-1713) 46

Quenet, Jean 46

Raymond, Simon 48

Ré Island, France 29

Richelieu River 29, 30, 32, 33, 38, 98

RICHER, Marguerite 49

ROBERGE *dit* Lacroix, Louis 101

ROBERT *dit* Lafontaine, Louis 35

ROBILLARD *dit* Lambert, Antoine   101

Rogers Rangers   64

ROLET, Marie   21

Roman Catholic   16, 44-46, 50, 61, 65, 67, 69

Rowney, David R.   61n

Royal American Regiment (60th Regiment)   64

Sabourin, Jean   16

Saguenay River region   21

Saint-Aubin-en-Bray, France   8, 20

Saint-Ours company, Carignan-Salières Regiment   29, 31, 98

Saint-Ours seigneury   33, 35, 98

Saint-Ours, Capt. Pierre   33, 98, 99

Saintonge, France   23

SAMSON, Amable Regis   101

Sandwich Township, Ont.   65, 66

Sandwich, Ont.   59, 66, 100

Santee Dakota Sioux (Isanyathi) ‡ — see Dakota Sioux

Sault St. Louis Mission   45, 46

Sault Ste. Marie   56

Saurel Company, Carignan-Salières Regiment   30

Sauvage, Françoise   61, 62

Sauvagesse, Dorothée (Wendat or Montagnais) ‡   19

Schenectady, NY   31

SEGUIN *dit* Laderoute, François   6, 8, 13, 20, 27, 28, 33-35,   — his descendants:
   Alfred - brother of Theodore   70
   Aline (Wanne) - daughter of Theodore & Alphonsine   3, 71, 72
   Andrea - daughter of Jerome   72
   Antoinette (Mailloux) - daughter of Theodore & Alphonsine   71, 72
   Arthur - son of Theodore & Alphonsine   71n
   Cajétan - son of Joseph (b.1694)   61
   Catherine - daughter of Leonard   71, 72
   Daniel Edward - son of Philip E.   72
   David - son of Jerome   72
   Donald - nephew of Theodore & Alphonsine   69
   Eustache - son of   69n, A-19
   Francis - son of Leonard   72
   Jean-Baptiste (b.1688) - son of Francois & Jeanne Petit   60

SEGUIN,
   Jean-Baptiste (b.1797) - great-grandfather of Theodore   101
   Jean-Baptiste (b.1798) - son of Joseph (b.1764)   66
   Jean-Baptiste - brother of Joseph (b.1764)   63
   Jeanne - daughter of Leonard   72
   Jeffrey - son of Roger   72
   Jerome - son of Theodore & Alphonsine   71, 72
   Joseph (b.1694) - son of Francois & Jeanne Petit   61, 62, 64
   Joseph (b.1717) - son of Jean-Baptiste (b.1688)   13, 59, 60, 61, 62, 64
   Joseph (b.1764) - son of Joseph (b.1717)   63, 64, 65, 69, 100
   Joseph (b.1829) - son of Jean-Baptiste (b.1798)   66, 68
   Kenneth - son of Leonard   71, 72
   Laurel Teresa - daughter of Philip E.   72
   Laurent - father of Francois   20
   Leonard - son of Theodore & Alphonsine   69, 70, 71, 72
   Marc Philip - son of Philip E.   72, A-13,
   Maria (Hammer) - sister of Alphonsine   70
   Matthew - son of Philip E.   72
   Napoleon - father of Theodore   3, 69
   Philip E. - son of Theodore & Alphonsine   69, 70n, 71, 72
   Philippe - father of Alphonsine   3, 67, 68
   Pierre - - son of Francois & Jeanne Petit   13
   Randall Arthur - son of Philip E.   72
   Renée - daughter of Leonard   72
   Robert - son of Leonard   71, 72
   Roger - son of Theodore & Alphonsine   71, 72
   Stephen - son of Jerome   72
   Suzanne - daughter of Leonard   72

Seguin, captain commanding a company of the Béarn Regiment   38n

Seguin, Jacques from Limoges, France   37, 37n

Seneca (Iroquois)   24, 30, 42

Seven Years War (French and Indian War, 1755-1763)   24, 36, 38, 39, 65

Ships — see *La Justice, La Nativité, Le Général, Le Joyeux Siméon, Le Saint André, Le Saint Siméon*

Siouan language   17

Sioux — see Dakota Sioux

Société de Notre Dame de Montréal   24, 26

Sorel, Que.   30, 44, 47

Spain   64
Spanish Netherlands (now Belgium)   50
St. Croix Island, Maine/New Brunswick border   21
St. Ignace Mission, Straits of Mackinaw   56
ST. JEAN *dit* Lavallée, Marie Madeleine ‡   16, 17
St. Joseph mission, Sillery, Que.   16
St. Joseph River, Michigan   57
St. Lawrence River   21, 24, 29, 30, 33, 35, 39, 41, 60
St. Lawrence valley   64, 65
St. Louis, Missouri   57
St. Nazaire, France   24
St. Pierre and Miquelon islands   65
St. Pierre Street, Tecumseh, Ont.   70
St. Simon and St. Jude church, Belle River, Ont.   69
Ste. Anne de Bellevue, Que.   46, 69
Ste. Anne's Roman Catholic church, Tecumseh, Ont.   67
Ste. Foy, Que.   39
Ste. Marie mission to the Wendat   55
Sulpicians   26, 56
SYLVESTRE, Marie — see OLIVIER, Marie ‡

TABEAU, Pierre   19
Tadoussac, Que.   19
TARDIF, Olivier   16
Tecumseh, Ont.   13, 66, 67, 70
Tecumseh Road, Windsor, Ont.   66, 67
Teiaiagon village (Toronto, Ont.) ‡   61
Terre Neuve — see Newfoundland
Thurso, Que.   13, 69
Tracy, Lieutenant-General Marquis Alexandre de Prouville   29-31, 33
Treaty of Paris 1763   39, 64
TREMBLAY, Marie Therese   61, 63, 64
Trois-Rivières, Que.   19, 24, 28, 35, 41, 44, 48, 56
Troupes de la Marine (*Compagnies Franches de la Marine*)   36-38, 42, 49, 50, 57
TUNÉ *dit* Dufresne, Marie Madeleine   57

Upper Country *(le Pays d'en Haut)*   18, 53-64
Ursuline nuns   16, 29, 53

VALIQUET *dit* Laverdure, Jean   48
VALIQUET, Marie Nicole   48
Varennes, Que.   39
Vaudreuil, Marquis Pierre Rigaud — governor of New France (1755-1760)   39
Vaudreuil, Que.   69
VERDON,
  Jean   49
  Marie Marguerite   49
VERONNEAU, Denis   35
Ville Marie - see Montreal
von Kreuzbourg's Jaeger Corps   39, 40

Wabanaki (Abenaki) ‡   16, 23, 24, 38, 41, 44, 45
Waite,
  Benjamin   44
  Canada   44
Walker, Hiram   67
Walkerville, Ont.   67, 70
Wanne,
  Allen   72
  Aline   3, 72
  Sidney   72
  Thomas   72
War of 1812 (1812-1814)   64, App. C
War of the Spanish Succession (Queen Anne's War, 1702-1713)   46
Wars of Religion, France (1562-1598)   50
Wellers Bay, Prince Edward County, Ont.   61
Wendat (Huron) ‡   16, 19, 23, 24, 41, 44, 55
Windsor, Ont.   59, 66, 69, 70
Winnebago (Hoocagra) ‡   54, 56
Wisconsin   41, 53, 56, 57
Wolfe, General James   39

York, Maine   45

www.ingramcontent.com/pod-product-compliance
Lightning Source LLC
Chambersburg PA
CBHW061112070526
44583CB00027B/3268